Restart

Getting Past Christian-ish

SCOTT L. ENGLE

CROSSBOOKS
PUBLISHING

CrossBooks™
A Division of LifeWay
1663 Liberty Drive
Bloomington, IN 47403
www.crossbooks.com
Phone: 1-866-879-0502

Some Scriptures taken from the Holy Bible, New International Version®,
NIV®. Copyright © 1973, 1978, 1984, 2011 by Biblica, Inc.™
Used by permission of Zondervan. All rights reserved worldwide. The
"NIV" and "New International Version" are trademarks registered in
the United States Patent and Trademark Office by Biblica, Inc.™

Some Scripture quotations are from the New Revised Standard Version Bible, ©
1989, Division of Christian Education of the National Council of the Churches of
Christ in the United States of America. Used by permission. All rights reserved.

A few Scripture quotations are from The Message. Copyright ©
by Eugene H. Peterson 1993, 1994, 1995, 1996, 2000, 2001,
2002. Used by permission of NavPress Publishing Group.

First published by CrossBooks 7/29/2013

ISBN: 978-1-4627-2867-1 (sc)
ISBN: 978-1-4627-2869-5 (hc)
ISBN: 978-1-4627-2868-8 (e)

Library of Congress Control Number: 2013910247

Printed in the United States of America.

This book is printed on acid-free paper.

Any people depicted in stock imagery provided by Thinkstock are models,
and such images are being used for illustrative purposes only.

Certain stock imagery © Thinkstock.

Table of Contents

To the staff and congregation of
St. Andrew United Methodist Church,
Plano, Texas

Preface

Although I've pretty much always been a churchgoer, only in recent years have I become a Christian. That might seem like an odd statement. But I've come to see that, for much of my life, I was what John Wesley called an "almost Christian." I went to church, sang in choir, taught Sunday school, sat on committees, and served as a lay speaker in the United Methodist Church. I studied the Bible and theology. I memorized Scripture. I tried to do right and to love mercy. Even so, it never made a real difference in my life, my world-view, or my sense of the future.

Yet by God's grace, I came to know what John Wesley learned in his mid-thirties: that I could spend my whole life as a nominal Christian, an "almost Christian," without ever truly putting my trust in God, without ever truly knowing that Christ died for me—yes, for the whole world, but also for *me*—without ever really knowing God, without ever really being one of God's people. Although I can still be plagued by doubts and uncertainties, as was Wesley, I now experience the joy of knowing and trusting God, the joy of God's love and forgiveness. Thankfully, God touched me and adopted me as one of his children. I will never be the same.

This business of "authentic Christianity" was unexplored territory for much of my family. I don't know why. But I think we were pretty typical. We grew up in an ostensibly Christian nation that taught us a faith well accommodated to the modern world. We learned a lot of things about Christianity, some of which were true but most of which were not, and based on this we made decisions. Some of us decided there was no intellectual basis for Christian belief. Some of us found churches that demanded so little that deeper faith issues could be easily ignored. And some of us simply found it easier to avoid the whole issue.

But Christianity cannot be ignored. Christians have been making extraordinary claims about all of reality for 2,000 years. Our story makes substantial, and at times shocking, demands of us all. For my part in this, I want to tell you something of why I believe as I do. I want to demonstrate that one can become a Christian without committing intellectual suicide. I want to challenge you to confront Christianity, as difficult or unnatural as that may seem. And I want to explain how most of us hold many wrong-headed notions about Christianity. But before we begin, there are a few things we need to get straight.

First, nothing here is original, as I am deeply indebted to the classical authors such as Augustine, Aquinas, Calvin, Luther, and Wesley, as well as modern-day thinkers and scholars, such as C.S. Lewis, Gordon Fee, Roger Olsen, Terence Fretheim, Richard Hayes, Michael Gorman, Dallas Willard and, in particular, N.T. Wright. In the footnotes, I will try to direct you to readings I've found especially helpful.

Second, I will presume you have little knowledge about Christianity, Judaism, or the Bible. This can be challenging because I also don't want to bore readers who have some background. My solution is to use footnotes to give supplemental information about the many actors and events in the story.

Third, I will strive to use the biblical texts responsibly. There will be no proof-texting,[1] since scriptural fragments can be used to support almost any notion. There will be no bumper sticker interpretation—the "God says it, I believe it, that settles it" sort of thing. Richard Hays reminds us that such misguided naiveté disrespects the very texts that the bumper sticker claims to support; interpretation is inescapable. Exactly what *does* God say? When I use quotations from the Bible, I will strive to include enough text to give a sense of the larger context. Beyond that, you'll have to trust that I will rely on thoughtful, informed, and contextual readings of the Bible,[2] bearing in mind that all readings of all texts are shaped, in part, by the mindset of the reader, though not so much as to prevent us from hearing the mind of the author.

Finally, we need to talk about vocabulary. When I taught university students, the more perceptive ones recognized that every course is a vocabulary course. If you are going to learn finance you must learn the vocabulary. Indeed, if you know the vocabulary of finance, then you know finance. Nobody goes

---

[1] Proof-text(ing) refers to the regrettable practice of assembling fragments of Scripture to support one's reading of the Bible, with no concern for the historical, literary, or canonical context of the fragments.

[2] For a brief and thoughtful presentation of these issues, see Richard B. Hays, *The Moral Vision of the New Testament* (New York: HarperCollins, 1996), 1-11. Hays' book isn't easy, but is enormously rewarding and challenging.

into a finance course thinking that vocabulary doesn't matter or that our best effort will get us close enough. Christianity has its own vocabulary. When Christians use words like faith, grace, sin, salvation, repentance, and wisdom, we use them in specific ways to convey specific notions. Further, Christians use these words differently from the rest of the world. Part of becoming a Christian is learning and living this vocabulary. In this book, I will try to use the vocabulary clearly, explaining what Christians mean when they use the words.

Acknowledgements

How do I possibly acknowledge all who have played a part in this book and the ministry that birthed it? I guess I'll just have to do the best I can.

First, of course, I want to thank my wife, Patti, without whose encouragement I would never have pursued the calling given me by God; indeed, without her, I might never have heard God's call. Without her help, not a word of this would have been written. Rather late in my life, God blessed me with an extraordinary and loving wife, and I will never be able to express fully the depth of my gratitude.

Second, I want to express my many thanks to Rev. Robert Hasley, the Senior Pastor of St. Andrew. For more than ten years now, Robert has inspired me and cheered me on, offering me opportunities to minister that would have been afforded me in very few other churches. I can never fully express my appreciation to Robert.

The incredible staff at St. Andrew has been with me every step of the way, never making me feel like I intruded on their work, although I'm sure I did, especially in those early days. What a wonderful and genuinely collegial team of Spirit-filled, hardworking ministers: Steve, Arthur, Amy, Charles, Chris, Edlen, Jay, Kay, Jennifer, Julie, Kate, and all the rest—thank you!

Many thanks to Connie Robertson, the assistant who helps me in all things and smiles each step of the way. She manages to remember everything I've forgotten.

My teaching ministry began with the encouragement of some who are no longer at St. Andrew: Rev. Kathryn Ransdell, now the Acting Lead Minister at St. Andrew's-Wesley United Church in Vancouver; Rev. Doug Meyer, now at Trietsch Memorial near Dallas; and Rev. Leighton Farrell, now with Christ, who was our Executive Pastor when I began my work. Leighton, who had been Senior Pastor at Highland Park UMC for twenty-five years, always made me more confident in my teaching and writing when I needed it the most.

Many thanks also to published authors Payne Harrison and Leroy Howe. They urged me to get a book out, and I'm sure they will be surprised to see that I finally did it.

Many thanks also to Kim Pierce, my editor. She has made this a more pleasurable reading experience for you … and for me.

Finally, but not last, many thanks to the congregation of St. Andrew. So many of you have been encouraging and loving over the years. By pushing me, you made me a better teacher, preacher, and Christian. You manage to ask the hard questions, but always with a smile. You inspire me and remind me always of the reasons I am in ministry. It seems like a fool's game to begin listing people, so I'll resist, although it is tempting. All of you mean more to me than you know.

And just one more: I have to acknowledge my indebtedness to N. T. Wright. Like many, I found my worldview reshaped in large part by the work of this gifted and prolific biblical scholar. Almost fifteen years ago, I picked up a copy of Wright's *The New Testament and the People of God*. Only later did I come to realize just how blessed I was to have found his work at the beginning of my ministry. My own book reverberates from beginning to end with what I have learned from him.

Restart?? Christian-ish??

I work at my computer a lot. Writing, preparing sermons and classes, researching, responding to e-mails, and so on. My computer chugs along pretty well until it begins to bog down, getting slower with every minute. Then ... I hit the Restart button in Windows 7 and all is made fresh and new again.

I think that many Christians are a bit like my computer. We might have started our Christian life with excitement and enthusiasm, we might have even grown up in the faith, but we find ourselves getting bogged down. Our Christian life becomes routine and even slipshod. We find ourselves going to church less and less often and getting less and less out of it. The lake beckons, or the soccer fields or the Sunday paper. We begin to think that just showing up on Sunday mornings is cause for praise. The church becomes little more than a bunch of nice people we like to see now and then. The Christian ethic becomes little more than being pleasant. And God becomes little more than a benign landlord who gets involved only when we think we need some help.

Lest you think I'm overdrawing the picture, the research backs me up. George Barna, a respected market researcher of all things Christian, consistently finds that those who profess to be Christian fall into two groups: (1) those for whom faith plays a very central role in their lives and (2) those for whom it does not. Based on his surveys, Barna identifies seven "faith tribes" in America.[3] Two of the "faith tribes" are Christian: he calls them Casual Christians and Captive Christians. The Casuals make up 80 percent of all who profess to be Christian and, thus, nearly two-thirds of all Americans.[4]

Similar results can be found in the work of Kenda Creasy Dean, Christian Smith and others[5] who have been analyzing and interpreting data from the National Study on Youth and Religion (NSYR), one of the most comprehensive and well done research projects on the sociology of religion. This study found that about 75 percent of American teenagers call themselves Christian and that most have followed their parents' religious beliefs and practices. For most of them, religion just isn't that big a deal; their religious beliefs can be summarized in the phrase "Moralistic Therapeutic Deism,"[6] referring to what is effectively a new religion that lives *within* Christianity. And, in this, these youth reflect their parents' beliefs and practices.

---

[3] From Barna's book, *The Seven Faith Tribes: Who They Are, What They Believe, and Why They Matter* (Carol Stream, Illinois: Tyndale House Publishers, 2009).

[4] Gallup, Barna, and other researchers find that roughly 80% of Americans label themselves as Christian

[5] See Kenda Creasy Dean's 2010 book, *Almost Christian: What the Faith of Our Teenagers is Telling the American Church* (US: Oxford University Press, 2010) and Christian Smith's (with Patricia Snell) 2009 book *Souls in Transition: The Religious and Spiritual Lives of Emerging Adults* (US: Oxford University press, 2009) for starters. Dean's book was chosen as *Christianity Today* magazine's 2010 book of the year in the category of Church and Ministry.

[6] Dean, p. 201-205

Dean and Smith summarize the beliefs of this new religion in this way:

1. A god exists who created and orders the world and watches over life on earth.
2. God wants people to be good, nice, and fair to each other, as taught in the Bible and by most world religions.
3. The central goal of life is to be happy and to feel good about oneself.
4. God is not involved in my life except when I need God to resolve a problem.
5. Good people go to heaven when they die.[7]

Granted, the name given this religion by the researchers, "Moralistic Therapeutic Deism (MTD)," is a bit cumbersome, but whatever name you give those guiding beliefs, it can't be "Christian." Yet, I'm pretty sure you could take the findings of the NSYR to virtually every pastor in America and each would nod knowingly. This is who is in the pews—and who is not. Indeed, the temptation to preach this MTD is pretty strong. It is what too many people come each Sunday wanting to hear: the Good News as little more than a vague "I'm Okay, You're Okay" therapy.

I should know all this, for I spent much of my life as a "casual Christian." Sure, I was in church most Sundays, but did it make a real difference in how I lived my life or saw the world around me? No. I suppose the problem was with what Michael Novak would call my "core convictions," the beliefs I truly

---

[7] Dean, p. 14

hold as reflected in how I live. I'm sure I publicly affirmed truly Christian beliefs and probably even convinced myself that I held those beliefs. But I would have been lying to myself. My core convictions were revealed in how I lived. It wasn't that I was some terrible person. I just didn't really shape my character or my life in response to anything distinctly Christian.

In this, I don't think I was that different from many (most?) of the people I went to church with. That all changed nearly fifteen years ago, when God moved in my heart and my life with great power. It is hard to describe, and I can't pinpoint this transformation to a specific time or place, only to a season. But it was real, very real.

Looking back, I can identify with John Wesley, who experienced a similar transformation. He went so far as to name the specific day and place: one evening as he sat in a chapel named Aldersgate listening to a sermon on the book of Romans (yes, really). He later said that he felt his heart "strangely warmed." At the time, Wesley was almost forty and had spent the better part of two decades in ministry. He had begun the movement that would be called "Methodism." He had been to Georgia in the American colonies as a missionary. Yet, he would describe that Aldersgate experience as the time when he moved from being what he called an "almost Christian" to an "altogether Christian." He knew that something important had changed in him and that he would never be the same. He knew that God had transformed his heart.

If you are a footnote reader, you probably noticed that Kenda Creasy Dean titled her book, *Almost Christian*, with Wesley's experience in mind. I prefer Dean's synonym, "Christian-ish." Wesley claimed that a person could have all the outward appearances of being Christian without having experienced the transformation and rebirth that comes with faith in Christ. And Dean's research confirmed this across a wide swath of America.

So right off, a few caveats:

1. *Can you know whether anyone else is merely "Christian-ish"?* No. Let me repeat that: No. This is not about helping you figure out who is and isn't an "authentic" Christian based on outward appearances. We are talking about an inner transformation, and only God knows the true state of anyone's heart.
2. *Can we at least know this about ourselves?* I'd submit even this can be difficult. If my experience and that of Wesley's is any guide, the best we can hope is that we will recognize transformation in ourselves after the fact.
3. *Can we do anything to transform ourselves from Christian-ish to Christian?* Nothing. Let me say that again: Nothing. The transformation of the heart is God's work, not ours. All the programs and studies we might join can't transform our hearts. All the sermons we hear. All the good deeds we might do. Transformation of the heart is God's work. This is hard for pastors and program leaders to hear, but it is the truth and has been part of orthodox Christian claims for 2,000 years.

All right, if we can't transform our own hearts … then is this about to be a very short book?

Nope. We can't transform our hearts; that is the work of the Holy Spirit. But we can make ourselves, as Dean puts it in her felicitous phrase, "highly combustible."[8] Yes, she says, we could spend our lives as a bunch of wet, green wood. We might catch fire. But why not make ourselves into dry kindling, ready to ignite when God's Spirit puts a match to us?

That's how I see Barna's "Casual Christians" or Dean's "Christian-ish." Good people. But wet, green wood. Heads and hearts filled with all kinds of misinformation and ignorance when it comes to the basics of the Christian faith. Not very combustible at all.

I've taught loads of educated, thoughtful, and well-meaning folks since my teaching and preaching ministry began at St. Andrew. Most hardly knew what they didn't know. Others thought they knew, but found themselves surprised time and again.

Let me give you an example: The Apostles' Creed has been affirmed by Christians in one form or another for nearly two millennia. Even churches that don't like creeds affirm these foundational beliefs. The last phrase in this simple creed is the affirmation of our belief in the "resurrection of the body and the life everlasting." But whose body are we talking about? Jesus' body? Our own? And if it is our own (as it is), then what

---

[8] You've probably realized that I think very highly of Dean's book. It is insightful and filled with lots of artful, eye-catching phrases. The first two chapters alone are worth the price of admission. The "church of benign." The "cult of nice." Great stuff.

does this mean for the life everlasting, for our notions of heaven and hell?

The fact is many people in the pews believe (if they even think about it) that they are talking about Jesus' body when they get to the end of the creed. That's my experience, from teaching thousands of them. Yet, the Christian proclamation that *all* of us will be bodily resurrected just as Jesus was resurrected has never been questioned in 2,000 years.

To make ourselves more combustible, we have to hit that Restart button. Go back to the basics and begin clearing away the fog that obscures from us the true nature of God and his work in this world and our lives. We have to "unlearn" a lot of well-meaning but misguided stuff.

This book is a good place to begin afresh. It is organized into three parts:

- *The basics of the overarching biblical story.* Many people know this bit and that bit from the Bible but lack a sense of the overarching narrative. They don't connect the dots. The first part should help with that.
- *The basics of Christian beliefs,* as expressed in the Apostles' Creed. This creed expresses the essentials on which all Christians have agreed from the beginning, and it avoids many of the differences that have arisen among us. Those differences matter, but the essentials on which we agree is the place to start—or Restart.
- *The basic criticisms.* The third part of the book will take a look at important and significant objections that we

often hear voiced about Christianity. Is God a bully? Is Jesus the only way? And more.

How to get the most out of this book

Don't underestimate the amount of fog-clearing that lies ahead. You may have hit that Restart button, but the reboot can be a pretty lengthy process. Don't rush it.

Be sure to read the Scripture passages. Each was chosen for a reason. Read through the passage and refer back to it. Even better, have your Bible open. Any of the modern translations will do (NIV, ESV, NRSV, and so on with the alphabet soup).

On your first time through a chapter, just read to get the overall picture. Then go back a second time, looking up references in your Bible and making a few notes to yourself.

If you are reading this as part of a small group, be sure to read the questions in the discussion guide that is available at www.scottengle.org. They're designed to provoke reflection. This stuff has to be taken in and chewed over. Scripture, too—chew on it, like a dog works over a bone,[9] and come back to it.

Finally, I didn't write this to be a read-it-and-put-it-away book. I mean it to be a resource to use as you strive to become ever

---

[9] Eugene Peterson has written an excellent book on reading the Bible, *Eat This Book* (Grand Rapids: Eerdmans Publishing Co., 2009), from which I got this memorable image of a dog and a bone.

more combustible. Keep it handy and come back to it from time to time. You might well get more out of later readings than from your first time through.

> Do not be conformed to this world, but be transformed by the renewing of your minds, so that you may discern what is the will of God—what is good and acceptable and perfect.
>
> (Romans 12:2)

PART I

The Biblical Story

Connecting Dots from Genesis to Revelation

The Bible

The Bible is not a book. It is a library of sixty-six books. Even those aren't really all "books." There are short stories, correspondence, essays, gospels, poetry, histories, prophecies[10], wisdom writings, apocalypses, and more.

The thirty-nine books of the Old Testament are often called the Hebrew Bible and were written in Hebrew. It is "the Bible Jesus read," as Philip Yancey, the popular Christian author, puts it. These books were written, edited, and compiled over many centuries, but by Jesus' day the content was settled.

The twenty-seven "books" of the New Testament were, on the other hand, written over a period of about fifty years, from AD 50 to AD 100.[11] Thirteen of the "books" are actually letters written by the apostle Paul in the course of his missionary work throughout the eastern Mediterranean. The New Testament was written in Greek.

As you begin to dig into your Bible, it is important to know that the division of the Bible into chapters and verses was done only about 800 years ago by a couple of Englishmen. Having

---

[10] By and large, the Bible's prophetic writings are not focused on foretelling the future, but *forth-telling* God's message for his people. The prophets are calling the people back to God and reminding them of the consequences of abandoning God.

[11] Jesus was crucified and resurrected in about AD 30.

numbered verses is helpful but dangerous, in that they encourage us to handle isolated verses while ignoring the context. Don't read verses in isolation—read the paragraph or, better, several paragraphs each side of the verse.

As with other writings, there are better and poorer ways to read the Bible. Some will get you closer the author's intent and, hence, God's. Some will take you further and further away from the truth of Scripture.

Richard Hays, a prominent New Testament scholar at Duke Divinity School, has suggested a simple method of getting to a sounder interpretation of Scripture.[12] I've used the method for years. It will serve you well.

There are four steps:

> *Read the text carefully*: Don't read into it what you expect to find. Read outwardly from it. Try to read it as the first readers would have. After all, the books of the Bible were written with ancient readers in mind.

> *Place the text in the context of all the rest of the Bible*: If you arrive at a new angle based on a single piece of the Bible, chances are you are heading down the wrong path. The larger biblical context will help to keep you on track.

---

[12] From Hays' book, *The Moral Vision of the New Testament* (New York: Harper Collins, 1996).

Relate the text to our situation: This is where you bring the passage forward to our day. This sometimes takes imagination, but imagination that is grounded by and tethered to the biblical story.

Live it! This is really the hard one, isn't it?

Beginnings—Acts 1 & 2

Genesis 1:1-5, 26, 3:1-13 (NIV)

In the beginning God created the heavens and the earth.
²Now the earth was formless and empty, darkness was over
the surface of the deep, and the Spirit of God was hovering
over the waters. ³And God said, "Let there be light," and
there was light. ⁴God saw that the light was good, and he
separated the light from the darkness. ⁵God called the light
"day," and the darkness he called "night." And there was
evening, and there was morning—the first day.

²⁶Then God said, "Let us make mankind in our image, in
our likeness, so that they may rule over the fish in the sea
and the birds in the sky, over the livestock and all the wild
animals, and over all the creatures that move along the
ground."

[God creates man and woman, Adam and Eve, and gives
them a beautiful garden in which to live and to work. God
tells them that the whole garden is theirs to enjoy with the
exception of the tree of the knowledge of good and evil. They
are not to eat the fruit of that tree, for God warns them that
if they do so, they will die.]

Now the serpent was more crafty than any of the wild
animals the Lord God had made. He said to the woman,
"Did God really say, 'You must not eat from any tree in the
garden'?"

² The woman said to the serpent, "We may eat fruit from the trees in the garden, ³ but God did say, 'You must not eat fruit from the tree that is in the middle of the garden, and you must not touch it, or you will die.' "

⁴ "You will not certainly die," the serpent said to the woman. ⁵ "For God knows that when you eat from it your eyes will be opened, and you will be like God, knowing good and evil."

⁶ When the woman saw that the fruit of the tree was good for food and pleasing to the eye, and also desirable for gaining wisdom, she took some and ate it. She also gave some to her husband, who was with her, and he ate it. ⁷ Then the eyes of both of them were opened, and they realized they were naked; so they sewed fig leaves together and made coverings for themselves.

⁸ Then the man and his wife heard the sound of the LORD God as he was walking in the garden in the cool of the day, and they hid from the LORD God among the trees of the garden. ⁹ But the LORD God called to the man, "Where are you?"

¹⁰ He answered, "I heard you in the garden, and I was afraid because I was naked; so I hid."

¹¹ And he said, "Who told you that you were naked? Have you eaten from the tree that I commanded you not to eat from?"

¹² The man said, "The woman you put here with me— she gave me some fruit from the tree, and I ate it."

¹³ Then the LORD God said to the woman, "What is this you have done?"

The woman said, "The serpent deceived me, and I ate."

*How well do you know the larger story of the Bible,
from Genesis to Revelation? It's time we begin connecting
the dots from beginning to end.*

In Part 1 of this book, we'll be looking at the overarching story of the Bible, from Genesis to Revelation. Yes, that's right. All in these few pages. Our purpose will be to see the larger story, to connect some dots, and to put even the story of Jesus in the larger story of God's work to restore his creation.

From my teaching over the years, I've discovered that most people have little idea how the larger biblical story works, even those who have spent time in Bible studies of one sort or another. Consequently, too many of us are left to puzzle through isolated stories that we hear in church or read about in a daily devotional. We have no way to connect them. Too often, they're reduced to finding a moral or a moment of inspiration. Here's an example: If someone asked you whether Jesus needed to be Jewish, how would you answer? Where would you put Jesus on the map of the Bible's story? Without answers to those questions and others, there is just no way to grasp the story of Scripture.

Here's a novel and useful way to tie the pieces together: Think of the larger biblical narrative as a six-act play[13]:

---

[13] I first encountered this way of teaching the story in the work of N. T. Wright, who used the metaphor of a five-act play with an epilogue. Later, Craig Bartholomew and Michael Goheen wrote a book, *The Drama of Scripture* (published by Baker Academic, 2004) built on Wright's structure, though they changed it to a six-act play. Their book is an excellent place to go for an in-depth treatment of the six-act play approach.

Act 1: God **creates** everything, including humans, in God's image

Act 2: The humans **rebel** against God, separating themselves from God and one another.

Act 3: God chooses and saves a people, **Israel**, through whom God will restore all humanity, indeed, all of creation.

Act 4: When Israel, God's people, proves unable to be faithful, God provides one faithful Israelite, **Jesus**, through whom God's restoration is achieved.

Act 5: God's renewal project continues as the Spirit of God empowers **the church** to build for the kingdom of God.

Act 6: Jesus returns and God's **restoration and renewal** is fully consummated in the arrival of the new heavens and earth.

Act 1: Creation

The story of Act 1, the beginning of it all, begins simply enough. God creates everything there is—yes, everything. If it exists, God created it. And God pronounces it all good. All of it. Every corner, every last bit and particle—good.

Of all the creatures that God creates, one is made in God's image: the humans. And God gives the humans the responsibility for God's good creation (Gen 1:26). That's what we mean by "stewardship" or "dominion."

We learn further that this good God creates a beautiful place for the humans, where they can live and work and love. In beautifully evocative imagery, we're told that God comes to walk with them in the evenings. There is even a tree in the garden from which the humans will eat so they will live in eternity with God. The humans are free to enjoy God, one another, and this garden—with one exception. There is one tree from which they are not to eat. If they do, God tells them, they will die, not live.

That's the big picture. God creates the cosmos and everything in it, and it is all good. When the curtain closes on the first act, there is nothing but hope and anticipation of the glories to come. But soon, a dark shadow falls across the stage.

Act 2: Rebellion

One thing. There is just one thing they should not do, one fruit they must leave uneaten. But they won't. A serpent approaches Eve and tells her that by eating the forbidden fruit of the tree of the knowledge of good and evil, she can know what God knows, i.e., she can be like God herself. Who among us could resist such a tantalizing promise? So Eve eats the fruit and then Adam does the same … and it all begins to plunge into ruin.

This act of rebellion, doing the one thing God asked them not to do, tears everything apart. Instead of walking with God in the evening, they hide from God, for shame has been planted in the garden. They point the finger at each other when God asks them what they have done. The relationships have been ripped apart; they are estranged from God and from each other.

And so God sends them out of the garden. They will not be able to eat from the tree of life and live forever; instead, they will now die. Death comes as a consequence of their sin, their act of separating themselves from God. As Paul wrote in his letter to the Romans, "For the wages of sin is death...." (6:23).

All the rest of the Bible is the story of God's work to put right what went so wrong in the Garden of Eden. The Bible is the story of God's rescue project.

The story of the fall,[14] as it is often called, is a sad story of human pride, imagining that we could be like God, that we could know what God knows. Indeed, the next major story in Genesis is Cain's murder of his brother, Abel. It is a short walk from rebellion against God to envy and murder. And it goes downhill from there.

---

[14] The label, the Fall, though commonly used by Christians, is actually derived from Plato. It describes the time, in Plato's conception, when immortal human souls fell from the world of the forms (true reality) to be imprisoned and encased in mortal bodies. Thus, death frees the immortal souls to return to the world of forms. In Plato, it is the place we are meant to be, our true home. That is most certainly not the Christian or the Jewish story.

To grasp the larger story of Scripture, we have to see God's larger purposes at work. Ever since the rebellion in the Garden, God has sought to rescue humanity and all of creation, to put right our relationship with God and our relationships with each other. Thus, for example, Jesus is asked for the most important teaching that God has given us. He responds that there are two: love God and love neighbor. In the Garden both were true—until Adam and Eve succumbed to pride and ate that forbidden fruit.

What about Noah?

The story of Noah and the flood in Genesis 6-9 is the story of a rescue attempt. Basically, God "uncreates," by means of the flood, and starts over with a new first family, that of Noah. Of course, pretty much as soon as they step off the ark, things go downhill; sin and shame are still with them. Soon, the humans build a tower to the heavens, the Tower of Babel. Why? So they can reach the heavens and walk where God walks. Sound familiar? So God knocks the tower down, scattering the people and their languages.

God's rescue project will have to proceed on a different course. We might be tempted to think that God would just wave his magic wand and make all things right. But love— and God *is* love (1 John 4:16)—is not a matter of magic but, instead, is about faithfulness, trust, and kindness. By their nature, all of these must be *freely* given. Even God cannot force or bribe someone to love him genuinely, for then it would not be love. A more pointed question might be this: Why doesn't God just walk away from the whole enterprise?

Why does God stick around and pursue relentlessly the rebellious and prideful humans? I suppose that the answer to that question takes us to a deeper understanding of the God who made us.

So … when the curtain comes down at the end of Act 2, a deep darkness has fallen across the story. Not only are the humans separated from God, they have fallen into murder, envy, hatred, and all the sins that plague us still. To make matters worse, as Paul writes in his letter to the Romans, all creation groans in labor pains. All creation awaits redemption.

From this point on, from the end of Act 2 forward, the Bible is one overarching story: the story of God's new way to put things right. God will come next to one man and one woman, Abram and Sarai, through whom God's work of salvation and redemption will move forward. Act 3 begins with their story and will take us all the way to Jesus.

A Bit More

The Truth about Sin

I remember leaving a St. Andrew worship service some years ago where I overheard a young woman say to her friend, "There was simply too much talk about sin today. That was such a downer." Those may not have been her exact words—I don't think young people actually use the word "downer" anymore—but her point was clear to me. The young woman didn't like to be told that there might be something wrong with her. Who does?

But if Christians are anything, we are realists. Rose-colored glasses have no place in our pockets. Sin is real and its presence explains a great deal about ourselves and our world. However, sin is commonly misunderstood. We tend to think of sin only as breaking a rule, as if we might look back over our day and count the sins we committed. But this is not the best way to go about understanding sin.

Sin is whatever separates us from God. Sin is whatever diminishes the image of God in us all. Sin is whatever keeps us from functioning as God intended. Sin is our brokenness—we are all broken—and we are often too blind to recognize it. Yes, we commit numerous sins, all the many ways we fail to love God and love others. But there is also "Sin," a beast within us that seeks to devour us, as God tells Cain in Genesis 4.

Adam, Eve, you, and I were all created by God so that we might love God and one another. When we chase after false gods or dishonor our parents or covet our neighbor's house or commit adultery, we are separated further and further from God. Adam and Eve, giving in to their pride and desiring to be like gods themselves, chose to follow their own way rather than God's way. The result: When God came to walk with them that evening, Adam actually hid from God ... *Separation.* The biblical story is about God's work to put back together what was torn apart that day in the garden.

Dominion and Stewardship

In Genesis 1:26, God gives the humans "dominion" (in the NRSV) over all the creatures of the planet. The Hebrew word here, *radah*, is most often translated "rule," as in to rule over. It is the authority held by kings. So the question then is this: What sort of rulers are we to be over this planet? And the answer to that question is straightforward. We are to exercise this dominion as Jesus, the King of Kings, rules. Jesus is to be our model of what it means to "rule" over the creatures of the earth.

That is why Eugene Peterson gets it just right in his paraphrase of 1:26 in *The Message*, when he uses the words "responsibility for" to render the Hebrew *radah*. As our king, Jesus has taken responsibility for us, as a shepherd for his sheep. Jesus showers us with care and with love. These are the images that ought to guide us as we exercise our responsibility for God's creation.

Stewardship is a word often used to convey this God-given responsibility for all that God has given us. In the New Testament, the image of humans being overseers or stewards of God's house is used ten times. But Leonard Sweet, a contemporary Christian theologian and futurist, suggests that "steward" is probably not the best way to think about this. After all, he notes, who really uses "steward" anymore, other than to refer to someone you might meet on a cruise ship

Instead, Sweet suggests that "trustee" is more meaningful for us and would be a better translation of the Greek. Many of us have some experience with trusts and the responsibilities held by trustees, even if only in connection with some sort of family estate. When we think of ourselves as God's trustees, the message of the Bible becomes clearer. We are given dominion over God's creation, not so we can rule as a tough or selfish taskmaster, but so we can be effective trustees of God's wealth, managing it wisely, helping it to grow and flourish. God's creation is not ours. We don't own it. Rather, we hold it in trust.

Likewise, we hold the Christian faith in trust and we are charged with guarding what has been entrusted to us (1 Tim. 6:20). God's people, the body of Christ, have received a treasure, a trust, given by the Holy Spirit (2 Tim. 1:14). This treasure is the truth about God and the proclamation that Jesus is Lord.

A Fresh Start—Act 3

Genesis 12:1-3, 15:1-6, 17:9-14 (NIV)

Now the LORD said to Abram, "Go from your country and your kindred and your father's house to the land that I will show you. ² I will make of you a great nation, and I will bless you, and make your name great, so that you will be a blessing. ³ I will bless those who bless you, and the one who curses you I will curse; and in you all the families of the earth shall be blessed."

After these things the word of the LORD came to Abram in a vision, "Do not be afraid, Abram, I am your shield; your reward shall be very great." ² But Abram said, "O LORD God, what will you give me, for I continue childless, and the heir of my house is Eliezer of Damascus?" ³ And Abram said, "You have given me no offspring, and so a slave born in my house is to be my heir." ⁴ But the word of the LORD came to him, "This man shall not be your heir; no one but your very own issue shall be your heir." ⁵ He brought him outside and said, "Look toward heaven and count the stars, if you are able to count them." Then he said to him, "So shall your descendants be." ⁶ And he believed the LORD; and the LORD reckoned it to him as righteousness.

⁹ God said to Abraham, "As for you, you shall keep my covenant, you and your offspring after you throughout their generations. ¹⁰ This is my covenant, which you shall keep, between me and you and your offspring after you:

'Every male among you shall be circumcised. [11] You shall circumcise the flesh of your foreskins, and it shall be a sign of the covenant between me and you."

Romans 4:1-5 (NIV)

What then shall we say that Abraham, our forefather according to the flesh, discovered in this matter? [2] If, in fact, Abraham was justified by works, he had something to boast about—but not before God. [3] What does Scripture say? "Abraham believed God, and it was credited to him as righteousness."

[4] Now to the one who works, wages are not credited as a gift but as an obligation. [5] However, to the one who does not work but trusts God who justifies the ungodly, their faith is credited as righteousness.

How will God put right all that was wrecked by humanity's rebellion in the Garden of Eden? God promises it will be fixed, that all creation will be restored and the humans' relationship with God will be reconciled.

Now we meet one man and one woman through whom God's great rescue project begins.

Recap

Act 1 is the story of creation. God creates everything there is and pronounces it all good. God also creates humans in God's own image and gives them responsibility for all the creatures of the earth. God gives the humans, a man and a woman, a beautiful garden in which to live and work. God even comes to walk with them in the evening. There are two special trees in this garden. The first is the Tree of Life, from which the humans will eat and, hence, live forever. The other is the Tree of the Knowledge of Good and Evil. God has warned the humans that they are not to eat of that tree or they will die.

When Act 2 opens, all is good and wonderful. The humans enjoy the relationship with God that God intended for them. But soon, it all falls apart. The woman is tempted to eat the forbidden fruit, believing that she will then know what God knows. She will be like a god herself. Sadly, she eats the fruit. The man follows suit and their relationship with God is torn apart. Rebellion against God has become their way. They hide from God and blame each other for what has happened. Tragically, they must leave the Garden and will never eat from the Tree of Life. They head off into exile. Soon, murder and other horrors become their way.

What's to be done? God "uncreates" with a flood and preserves a single family who will start over. But it goes no better. Eventually, the humans build a tower to the heavens, so that they can walk where God walks, just as the humans in the garden wanted to know what God knows.

Thus, when the curtain falls on the second act, a deep and foreboding silence has fallen across the stage. What is to be done? More to the point, what will God do? The humans are still estranged from God and one another. All of God's creation still groans under the weight of rebellion and pride. What is the cure for the curse? Where is the repair for the rupture? How will God put things right so that love, mercy and justice are the way of life?

Act 3—A Fresh Start

In Acts 1 and 2 (Gen. 1-11), we encountered a Tree of Life and a boat big enough to carry two of each species on the planet. We met a talking serpent and the Nephilim. We saw a cherubim standing guard over a garden and rain falling at the rate of fifteen feet per hour.

But all that changes when we come to Genesis 11:27, when we are thrust into the story of a family that can, at times, be uncomfortably like our own. When Act 3 opens we find ourselves in the world of the ancient Near East, a world and a time that can be reached by historians and archaeologists. It is nearly 4,000 years ago. Granted, a long time when measured by the span of our lives, but we know about civilizations much older. The Great Pyramid of Egypt had stood for more than 700 years by this time. It is the time of Hammurabi of Babylonia and his extensive written legal code.

In this ancient, but knowable, world we meet a man named Abram.[15] He and his family live in Haran, far to the north of

---

[15] Later in the book of Genesis, Abram will be given a new name by God. "Abraham" means something like "father of a multitude." The name of Abram's wife, Sarai, will be changed to Sarah. God changes Abram's name when God tells Abram that circumcision of male children is to be a sign of the covenant between God and Abram. In ancient cultures, a new name would signify a new phase in the person's life.

Canaan,[16] his father having moved there from Ur. One day, God speaks to Abram. There is no fanfare, no burning bush, no angels or flaming swords. Just a guy and the Creator of the Cosmos.

There is nothing distinctive about Abram. God could have chosen anyone through whom to begin the restoration of all creation. But he chose Abram. Abram, later called Abraham, would become the father, the patriarch, of God's people.

Three promises

God makes three promises to Abram when he comes to him that day and later:

- God will give him a land.
- God will make Abram's family a great nation, more numerous than the stars.
- All the families of the earth will be blessed through Abram.

There does seem to be one problem with God's plan. Abram and his wife, Sarai, are old, really old. Sarai is far past child-bearing years. But, God promises them a family and it is a family they will get. All is possible with God.

---

[16] Canaan is the ancient name of the land that would become the homeland of biblical Israel, given to them by God. Later, it would come to be called Palestine. The people living in this area in the time of Abraham were known as the Canaanites.

People focus on the first two promises, perhaps because they are so dramatic, so much so that the third promise gets forgotten and overlooked. Yet, I can't overstate its importance. God's call of Abraham sets the stage for all that follows. Yes, Abraham will become the father of a great nation. Yes, he will go to the land given him by God. But, more importantly, "all the families of the earth shall be blessed" through Abraham. In the Old Testament, blessing is a gift from God, encompassing material well-being, peace, and success in life. Blessing shapes the lives of Abraham's family and the "outsiders" they meet. Such blessing will be brought to all the people of the earth. *The accomplishment of this blessing is God's larger purpose in the biblical story.*

As Act 3 rolls on, the Israelites will often forget that Abraham was not chosen by God merely for his own sake, nor even merely for theirs, but for the sake of the whole world. Later, when God rescues the Hebrews from Egypt, it is for the sake of all humanity and every corner of creation.[17] It will always be easy for the Israelites to forget that they were to build, even to be, the city on the hill to which all nations would stream (Isaiah 2:2-5; Matthew 5:14-16). It was tempting to them, as it is tempting to us, to turn inward, to build barriers, to see people as "outsiders." Jesus would remind his fellow Jews that they were to be the "light to the world." If we are going to understand the larger biblical story, we have to keep

---

[17] The book of Ruth is an excellent example. It tells the story of a young Moabite woman, i.e., not an Israelite and not a descendent of Abraham, who through her Israelite mother-in-law, is blessed by God and incorporated into God's people. She goes on to become the great grandmother of King David, the greatest of all Israel's kings.

God's larger purpose in mind—namely, putting right what was ruined by the rebellion in the Garden of Eden.

A sign of this covenant

So, as odd as it seems, God's great rescue plan begins with one man and one woman, Abram and Sarai. And God gives them a sign of God's promises. All the males of this growing family are to be circumcised, including infants at birth. This practice of circumcision is to mark them as the people of God. It functions like a badge of membership among God's people.[18]

It is not that the circumcision is a condition for God to keep his promises. Rather, circumcision is an outward sign, a baptism of sorts into the family through whom God is working in a special and focused way. There is no deal on the table, just God's promises. There is no Law, no Ten Commandments, no priests, no tabernacle, and no sacrifices. All that will come later in Act 3. For now, God simply makes profound and surprising promises to Abraham.

The child and the family

Though Sarah is long past her child-bearing years, God gives them a son, Isaac. Isaac's sons are Esau and Jacob. Jacob has

---

[18] Circumcision was such a powerful badge of membership that, in Jesus' day, there were Jewish men who, seeking to be more acceptable in the Greco-Roman culture, underwent an operation to "undo" their circumcision cosmetically. Referring to circumcision and other markers of faith as badges of membership is one of many helpful phrases from N. T. Wright.

twelve sons who become the fathers of the twelve tribes of Israel.[19] The stories of this family across the generations occupy the rest of the book of Genesis. There is much we learn about God in these stories, but Abraham and his family certainly are not always models of faithfulness. Far from it. Indeed, even betrayal and murder plague the family. Yet, through it all, God's purpose, this large rescue project, moves forward even when we have difficulty discerning how this could be.

By the opening of the book of Exodus, the people of God are so vast a number that, although they are enslaved, Egypt's Pharaoh is frightened of them. God would choose Moses to lead his people out of slavery and back to Canaan, where God would be their king, though not for long. And so the story continues for centuries. Through it all, God would relentlessly pursue his people, calling them back to the love of God and neighbor, rescuing them, and always preserving a remnant of the faithful, a nucleus of his redeemed and chosen people.

---

[19] I've learned from my classes that the term "Israel" can be confusing. "Israel" was the collective name of the twelve tribes descended from Jacob, Abraham's grandson. After spending a night wrestling with a stranger who turns out to be God, Jacob was given the name "Israel," which in Hebrew means something like "one who strives with God." From that time on, the name "Israel" would not only designate the ancestor Jacob, but also God's people, as in the twelve tribes "of Israel." Later, it would take on national and political meaning as well. Thus, David would be King of Israel. Your reading of the Bible will be helped by keeping in mind that "Israel" sometimes refers to the people of God and at other times refers to a kingdom.

A man of faith

As we go forward in Act 3 through all the stuff about the Law, the priests, and the rest, it's be easy to lose sight of the truth that God's plan will progress on the basis of faith. It was about faith with Abraham, and it is still about faith.

Abraham's story is not only foundational to all that follows in the history of God and his people, Abraham demonstrated his trust of God time after time.

- God tells Abraham to leave his home and family to go to Canaan and he goes.
- God tells Abraham that he will have numerous descendents, despite the fact that Abraham and Sarah are both approaching the century-mark. "And he believed the Lord; and the Lord reckoned it to him as righteousness" (Gen. 15:6).
- God tells Abraham to sacrifice the son born to himself and Sarah, the child through whom the covenant will pass. Though God stops him from this killing, Abraham offers his son to God, knowing that God could and would, figuratively, raise the boy from the dead. Abraham trusts God even in this.

When the writer says that God reckoned Abraham's faith to him as righteousness (in 15:6), it is a way of saying that Abraham's faith enabled the restoration of God and Abraham's relationship. Notice that this pivotal statement about Abraham's faith having put him right with God comes *before* Abraham is given the sign of circumcision in Genesis 17.

Nearly two millennia after Abraham, Paul wrote a letter to the Christians in Rome. He wanted them to understand that with God it had always been about faith, going all the way back to Abraham. It was faith, and faith alone, that restored Abraham to a right relationship with God, not circumcision or Sabbath-keeping or any of the other "works of the law" that would come later.

Thus, Paul uses Genesis 15:6 to demonstrate that righteousness was Abraham's by virtue of his faith, even before God taught him the rite of circumcision as a sign of the covenant. And it happens centuries before the Law was brought down from the mountain by Moses. Thus, even the Law of Moses (more on this in the next chapter) could not be the basis of a restored relationship with God. That happens through faith. And it is a faith available to *everyone*, to all the families of the earth, not merely those who were given the Law.

Abraham was not Jewish when God made his promises to him. He was uncircumcised and did not have the Law. He was just a guy. A guy who trusted his Lord. It was this trust that proved the wisdom of God's choice. It was always about this faith and trust. Faith would be the means by which God's promise to Abraham would be extended to all the families of the earth. It is our own faith in Jesus that marks us out as God's people.

In the next chapter, we come to the story of the Exodus, the time when God saved his people from slavery in Egypt. God will give his people the Law and instruct them on building a suitable place for God to dwell with them. But through it all, it will be a story about faith.

The God Who Saves—Act 3 Continued

Exodus 3:1-6; 19:1-6 (NIV)

[God's people, the descendants of Abraham, have been in Egypt for several hundred years and enslaved by the Egyptians. But God is riding to the rescue and begins this mission by coming to an Israelite named Moses, who has fled Egypt after murdering an Egyptian foreman.]

Now Moses was tending the flock of Jethro, his father-in-law, the priest of Midian, and he led the flock to the far side of the wilderness and came to Horeb, the mountain of God. ² There the angel of the LORD appeared to him in flames of fire from within a bush. Moses saw that though the bush was on fire it did not burn up. ³ So Moses thought, "I will go over and see this strange sight—why the bush does not burn up."

⁴ When the LORD saw that he had gone over to look, God called to him from within the bush, "Moses! Moses!"

And Moses said, "Here I am."

⁵ "Do not come any closer," God said. "Take off your sandals, for the place where you are standing is holy ground." ⁶ Then he said, "I am the God of your father, the God of Abraham, the God of Isaac and the God of Jacob." At this, Moses hid his face, because he was afraid to look at God.

[God comes to Moses and sends him to confront Pharaoh and demand that the Hebrews be set free. After much trouble and tragedy, that comes to pass and the people cross the Red

Sea. They make their way to the mountain where Moses had first met God.]

On the first day of the third month after the Israelites left Egypt—on that very day—they came to the Desert of Sinai. ²After they set out from Rephidim, they entered the Desert of Sinai, and Israel camped there in the desert in front of the mountain.

³ Then Moses went up to God, and the LORD called to him from the mountain and said, "This is what you are to say to the descendants of Jacob and what you are to tell the people of Israel: ⁴ 'You yourselves have seen what I did to Egypt, and how I carried you on eagles' wings and brought you to myself. ⁵ Now if you obey me fully and keep my covenant, then out of all nations you will be my treasured possession. Although the whole earth is mine, ⁶ you will be for me a kingdom of priests and a holy nation.' These are the words you are to speak to the Israelites."

1 Samuel 8:4-9 (NIV)

[Long after fleeing Egypt, the Israelites have conquered the land of Canaan, which God promised to Abraham, and have settled there. It has not gone well, as the people have demonstrated their faithlessness time and again. Now, even though God has always been their king, they are insisting upon a human king. God's prophet, Samuel, warns them about the dangers of such kings.]

⁴ So all the elders of Israel gathered together and came to Samuel at Ramah. ⁵ They said to him, "You are old, and

your sons do not follow your ways; now appoint a king to lead us, such as all the other nations have."

⁶ But when they said, "Give us a king to lead us," this displeased Samuel; so he prayed to the LORD. ⁷ And the LORD told him: "Listen to all that the people are saying to you; it is not you they have rejected, but they have rejected me as their king. ⁸ As they have done from the day I brought them up out of Egypt until this day, forsaking me and serving other gods, so they are doing to you. ⁹ Now listen to them; but warn them solemnly and let them know what the king who will reign over them will claim as his rights."

Who is this God who makes such extravagant promises? Can he really be trusted? God has chosen a people, but will he now remember them and save them?

Recap

God creates everything, including humans, in God's image. All is good until the humans rebel against God, seeking to be like gods themselves. This rebellion not only destroys the humans' relationship with God but even damages God's creation. Thus end Acts 1 and 2.

So, at the beginning of Act 3, God launches a project of restoration and renewal, choosing one couple, Abraham and Sarah, through whom this work will proceed. God promises them a land to call their own, descendants more numerous than the stars, and, most importantly, that all the families of the earth will be blessed through them.

Though Sarah is long past her childbearing years, God gives them a son, Isaac. Isaac's sons are Esau and Jacob. Jacob has twelve sons who become the fathers of the twelve tribes of Israel. When a famine comes upon the land of Canaan, Jacob's sons are driven to Egypt. There they stay and are eventually enslaved by the Egyptians.

God's people are in desperate need of rescue. So God chooses one man, Moses, who will be God's prophet, the one to lead God's people out of Egypt. This is the story of the Exodus.

The Exodus

When the book of Exodus opens, Abraham's descendants (through Isaac, Jacob, and Jacob's twelve sons) have been enslaved in Egypt for several hundred years. Sometime around 1500-1300 BC, Moses is born, grows up in the Pharaoh's house, murders an Egyptian who was beating a fellow Hebrew, and disappears into the desert. There, he marries and tends to his flocks.

One day, he sees a bush that is burning but is not consumed by the fire. When he investigates, Moses is confronted by God, who tells Moses that God is going to save the Hebrews. It is in this meeting that God reveals his name to Moses: YHWH, which means "I am" or "I am who I am" (Exodus 3:1-6).

Moses resists and offers up some reasons why he isn't the right guy, but God persists. Eventually, Moses, with the help of his brother, Aaron, returns to Egypt to confront the Pharaoh and demand freedom for the Hebrews. As you'd expect, the

Pharaoh resists, so God sends plague after plague upon Egypt. In the end, Pharaoh relents only when God sends death to strike all the first-born of Egypt. However, the death passes over the homes of the Hebrews who have marked their doorways with the blood of a lamb.[20]

After this final plague, Pharaoh lets the Hebrews go, but then changes his mind and chases after them. God parts the Red Sea (or "sea of reeds") to let the Hebrews pass, but the Egyptian army is drowned when they follow the Hebrews into the parted waters.

God then leads the Hebrews into the desert. After a few months, they arrive at Mt. Sinai where God gives Moses the Ten Commandments and the instructions for building God's tabernacle, the place where God will dwell with his people. God also instructs the people on a system of priests and sacrifices that will mark them out as God's people.

God comes to his people

Though the plagues in the Exodus story capture people's imagination, the heart of the story is the encounter between God and his people at Mount Sinai. There, Moses climbs the mountain to appear before God, who reminds the people of

---

[20] Jews commemorate this "passing over" every spring. In the last week before his crucifixion, Jesus arrived in Jerusalem for the Passover celebration. The last supper of Jesus and his disciples was a Passover dinner. Thus, the followers of Jesus came to see him as the Passover lamb, who was essentially inaugurating a new Exodus. This, Jesus was seen the one whose sacrificial death makes our own salvation possible.

what God has done for them and then proposes a covenant with the Israelites: "If you will obey me and keep my covenant, you will be my special treasure" (see Exodus 19:1-6). When Moses returns from the mountain, the leaders of the people meet and agree to accept the covenant, "to do everything Yahweh asks of us." After everything God had done for them, the Israelites' willingness to accept God's covenant shouldn't surprise us. Sadly, neither will their failure to keep it.

After the people accept the covenant with God, the most amazing thing happens. God tells Moses that he will come to the people in a cloud of smoke so they can hear the audible voice of God! God is going to spell out clearly the terms of the covenant Israel has accepted so that all can hear. Thus, Moses assembles the people at the base of the mountain where God, in smoke and fire and announced by the blowing of a ram's horn, addresses his people.

Instruction in the covenant

In God's address, YHWH lays out a series of ten terse commandments. In these commandments, God begins to shape a people who will be holy, who will reflect God's own character. The Ten Commandments begin God's instruction on how to live in right relationship with God and with one another. This entire passage (Exodus 20-31) is foundational to the biblical narrative, and there are at least three keys to understanding why this is so.

First, God's choosing and saving of Israel was never simply for their own sake but for the sake of the whole world. Looking back from Mount Sinai, the Israelites can remember God's promise to Abraham that all nations would be blessed through him (Genesis 12:3). More than a thousand years later, Jesus would remind his disciples that they were to be the light to the world and not hide their light under a bushel basket (Matthew 5:14-16). But to be the light to the world, to be the ones through whom God would restore all creation, God's people had to grow in holiness. Their character had to reflect God's own character. The Ten Commandments begin to show the Israelites what it means to love God and to love neighbor. The abstract commandment to love is made concrete by the commandments.

Second, God is going to dwell with his people. But just how does a holy God live with an unholy people who remain very much the children of the rebellious and disobedient Adam?[21] So, in Exodus 25, God gives them instructions for building a tabernacle[22], a moveable shrine in which God will dwell. The Israelites didn't imagine that God could be contained in a tent, but they knew that God's presence would be with them in a way that he was not with other peoples. God would dwell

---

[21] We are all children of Adam in the sense that we are all sinful, failing to love fully God and our neighbor. It is the separation and estrangement created by "sin" that must be fixed.

[22] The tabernacle was a moveable tent, suitable for a nomadic people. Inside was a place set apart from the rest that was called the Holy of Holies. In it was kept the Ark of the Covenant containing the stone tablets brought down the mountain by Moses. Centuries later, when the people were settled in the Promised Land, they would build a permanent temple in Jerusalem. It was patterned on the tabernacle described in the book of Exodus.

with *them*! Imagine that God came to you and told you that he would live upstairs in your home. What a privilege; what a responsibility.

Third, God sets up a system of rituals, priests, sacrifices, and festivals so that the people can begin to learn that some things are holy and some are not. They must learn that the two do not mix. The priestly system teaches the people that God cannot be approached by a sinful and unholy people. Thus, the priests and sacrifices accomplish, after a fashion, the reconciliation of God and his people. But still, all the rituals, priests, and sacrifices are only signposts to the real thing; they could never be the "real thing" itself. That will await the arrival of God's own son (Act 4).

Israel breaks the covenant

In the midst of the Exodus story, we learn that the people will be unable to live up to their end of the bargain. While Moses is on the mountain with God, the people start whining, even wishing they were back in Egypt. And when they decide that Moses isn't coming back, they fashion a calf made of gold, an idol, and thank this figurine for saving them from Pharaoh. It boggles the mind, but this story would be repeated countless times in the pages of the Old Testament.

After leaving the mountain

After leaving Mount Horeb/Sinai, God leads his people to the land God had promised to Abraham. They send spies into Canaan to check things out and, being terrified by what they see, the people turn back. Rather than trusting in God, they trust in their own judgment. As you might expect, God is angry with them and tells them that they will not enter the Promised Land until that entire generation dies.[23] Even Moses will never enter Canaan. Thus, the Hebrews wander aimlessly in the wilderness for forty years.[24] The book of Deuteronomy then is largely Moses's final speech to the new generation of the Hebrews, who will soon begin their conquest of Canaan. Moses's death is recorded at the end of Deuteronomy.

Settling in Canaan—the time of the judges

Under God's leadership and that of Joshua, the Israelites crossed the Jordan River and entered Canaan, the land promised to Abraham centuries before. After the Israelites conquered large portions of Canaan, they settled into a long period of consolidation. The book of Judges tells the story of this very difficult, indeed tragic, period in Israel's history.

Unlike the peoples around them, the Israelites did not have a human king, for God was to be their king. The leadership and administration of the twelve tribes was handled by men and women known as "judges." Generally, the judges of Israel were

---

[23] Two of the spies, Joshua and Caleb, urge the people to trust in God's promises and enter the land, but they are ignored. Because of their faithfulness to God, Joshua and Caleb are allowed to lead the next generation into Canaan.

[24] This time in the wilderness becomes an important theme in the Bible. For example, where does Satan tempt Jesus after his baptism? In the wilderness.

chosen from among the heads of the twelve tribes. They had the authority to settle disputes and promote justice. They also provided military leadership.

As we might expect, some of the judges were "minor" and of little note. But others were lauded by Israel as saviors who led the tribes in times of crisis when the existence of Israel was threatened. For example, Othniel was the first judge and is presented in the book of Judges as an ideal leader who rescues the Israelites from oppression. Other judges are better known, such as Deborah, Gideon, and Samson. Deborah was not only the legal and military leader of Israel, she was also a prophet. She must have been a remarkable woman, given the patriarchal nature of the ancient world.

Although God raised up many judges who led the people back to God, their faithfulness was inevitably short-lived. Succeeding generations would fall further and further away from God, until God raised up yet another judge. It could be described as descending cycles of faithlessness. In the end, the people abandoned God's way entirely, doing "what was right in their own eyes" (Judges 21:25).

No king but God?

The book of Samuel[25] begins with the story of the man who would be the last of Israel's judges and the first of many writing

---

[25] The books of 1 and 2 Samuel are one writing, as is 1 and 2 Kings and 1 and 2 Chronicles. They were too lengthy to fit on a single scroll, hence the tradition of dividing the books in two. This is *not* true of New

prophets. The Israelites' clamor incessantly for a king, a human king, so that they can be like the nations around them. This is a rejection of God, for up until now God has been their king.

Though God, speaking through Samuel, warns them that they are not going to be happy with human kings, who are takers, the people insist and God relents. Samuel anoints a man named Saul as the first king of the united kingdom of Israel. David will be the second king and Solomon the third.

Looking ahead

In the next chapter, we'll look at the story of Israel's kings and the unwillingness of the people to be faithful to God, leading to their exile in Babylonia. We'll examine their return to Jerusalem, such as it was, and the centuries they spent under foreign rule—right up to the time a baby is born to a virgin in Bethlehem.

Testament books like 1 and 2 Corinthians, which are two different letters from Paul.

A Bit More

Covenants

The notion of covenant is one of the central themes of the Bible. It isn't a word we use much anymore, but it expresses the making and keeping of commitments and promises. An excellent example today is a marriage covenant.

Although there are several types of covenants in the Bible, they fall into two broad categories: (1) the covenant between God and his people and (2) the covenants among humans.

Covenants are used in the Bible to bind two persons legally and personally, as when Jonathan makes a covenant with David (1 Samuel 18:3-4), wherein their loving bond diminishes the legal aspects of the covenant. In other cases, such as the covenant between Laban and Jacob (Genesis 31:43-54), the legal power of the covenant is much more important because Laban and Jacob don't trust each other. In most biblical covenants between humans, God is called on as the witness and guarantor.

When God is a participant in the covenant, such as God's covenants with Noah (Genesis 9:8-17) or Abraham (12:1-3) or Moses (in Exodus and Deuteronomy) or David (see 2 Samuel 7), the covenant takes on all the theological significance of a commitment between God the creator and his creation, between God the king and his people.

Jesus, the Law, and the Two Tablets

When Moses came down from Mount Sinai, he brought two tablets containing what we call the Ten Commandments. These commandments can be found in Exodus 20. The first four commandments speak to our relationship with God: do not worship any other God, don't make idols, don't abuse God's name, keep the Sabbath holy. The last six speak to our relationship with others: honor your parents, don't murder, don't commit adultery, don't steal, don't testify falsely against your neighbor, and don't covet other people's possessions. The Ten Commandments lie at the heart of the Old Testament law.

Many people mistakenly believe that Jesus came to abolish the Old Testament Law. On the contrary, Jesus came to fulfill the law. In his Sermon on the Mount, Jesus taught his disciples what God's Law is really all about. When tested by the young lawyer, Jesus said that all the Law can be summed up in the commandments to love God (the first tablet) and to love neighbor (the second tablet). All of the ethical "do's and don'ts" one finds in the Bible are simply concrete expressions of the two commandments to love.

God's Relentless Pursuit—still Act 3!

1 Kings 11:1-8 (NIV)

King Solomon, however, loved many foreign women besides Pharaoh's daughter—Moabites, Ammonites, Edomites, Sidonians and Hittites. ² They were from nations about which the LORD had told the Israelites, "You must not intermarry with them, because they will surely turn your hearts after their gods." Nevertheless, Solomon held fast to them in love. ³ He had seven hundred wives of royal birth and three hundred concubines, and his wives led him astray. ⁴ As Solomon grew old, his wives turned his heart after other gods, and his heart was not fully devoted to the LORD his God, as the heart of David his father had been. ⁵ He followed Ashtoreth the goddess of the Sidonians, and Molek the detestable god of the Ammonites. ⁶ So Solomon did evil in the eyes of the LORD; he did not follow the LORD completely, as David his father had done.

⁷ On a hill east of Jerusalem, Solomon built a high place for Chemosh the detestable god of Moab, and for Molek the detestable god of the Ammonites. ⁸ He did the same for all his foreign wives, who burned incense and offered sacrifices to their gods.

Hosea 2:13-20 (NRSV)

¹³ I will punish her for the festival days of the Baals, when she offered incense to them and decked herself with her

ring and jewelry, and went after her lovers, and forgot me, says the LORD.

¹⁴ Therefore, I will now allure her,
and bring her into the wilderness,
and speak tenderly to her.
¹⁵ From there I will give her her vineyards,
and make the Valley of Achor a door of hope.
There she shall respond as in the days of her youth,
as at the time when she came out of the land of Egypt.

¹⁶ On that day, says the LORD, you will call me, "My husband," and no longer will you call me, "My Baal." ¹⁷ For I will remove the names of the Baals from her mouth, and they shall be mentioned by name no more. ¹⁸ I will make for you a covenant on that day with the wild animals, the birds of the air, and the creeping things of the ground; and I will abolish the bow, the sword, and war from the land; and I will make you lie down in safety. ¹⁹ And I will take you for my wife forever; I will take you for my wife in righteousness and in justice, in steadfast love, and in mercy. ²⁰ I will take you for my wife in faithfulness; and you shall know the LORD.

We come to the closing scenes of Act 3. Sadly, the Israelites' faithlessness is demonstrated time and again. Yet, the Lord God, the lover of his people, relentlessly pursues them, unwilling to let them go.

Our story so far

In Acts 1 and 2 of our play, the humans were created by God and then rebelled against God. We might think that would be the end of the story. God would move and that would be that.

But God sticks around, desiring to reconcile his beloved humans to himself, to put things right, to restore all of creation to the promise it once held. So, at the beginning of Act 3, God launches a project of restoration and renewal, choosing one couple, Abraham and Sarah, through whom this work will proceed. God promises them their own land, a huge family, and that all of humanity would be blessed through them.

Abraham and Sarah eventually have a son, Isaac, who has twin sons of his own, Esau and Jacob. Jacob has twelve sons who become the fathers of the twelve tribes of Israel. When a famine comes upon the land of Canaan, Jacob's sons are driven to Egypt. There they stay and are eventually enslaved by the Egyptians. God's people are thus in desperate need of rescue. In the previous chapter, we saw how God saved his people, through Moses, liberating them from their Egyptian masters and entering into a binding covenant with them.

1,000 years of history

The Old Testament can be intimidating with all the strange names, places, and just plain weirdness. In this short chapter, we'll look at more than a thousand years of Israel's history. This may seem overwhelming, but in the larger sense, the story of Israel is rather simple. So here goes.

After the death of Moses, Joshua led the Israelites in a war of conquest, occupying much of the land of Canaan. Over a couple of hundred years, the Israelites consolidated their conquests and settled large portions of the Promised Land.[26] During this period, the Israelites were governed by judges; people such as Deborah, Samson, and Samuel who guided Israel under God's kingship. But the book of Judges paints a rather bleak picture of the inability of God's people to live under God's Law. As the last verse of the Book of Judges puts it, everyone in that time did what was right in their own eyes.

God had given his people judges because he did not want Israel to have an earthly king. God himself was to be their king. However, God's people kept demanding a king such as their neighbors had and God finally relented, anointing Israel's first king, Saul.

There were only three kings of a united Israel—Saul, David, and David's son, Solomon. Saul was a disappointment, but David was to become Israel's greatest king, the person whom Israel would always see as the idealized king of Israel.[27] Solomon ruled at a time when Israel reached the peak of its political power and wealth, enabling Solomon to build the temple that stood for more than 400 years. But Solomon also planted the seeds of Israel's eventual destruction, for he allowed the worship of foreign gods.

---

[26] If you have a study bible, the maps in the back will probably help you see what is going on in Israel's history.

[27] David was king of united Israel in roughly 1000 BC.

After Solomon's death in 922 BC, Israel split into two kingdoms. The ten northern tribes formed themselves into a kingdom that called itself Israel. The two tribes that lived in the south, the tribes of Judah and Benjamin, formed themselves into a kingdom called Judah. The story of these two kingdoms, Israel in the north and Judah in the south, are told in parallel in the book of Kings (1 and 2).

Beginning with Samuel, God sent prophets to his people during the time of the kings and after. For more than 500 years, these prophets would bring God's word to the people, calling them back to God, warning of the consequences if they did not, and offering words of hope from a gracious and merciful God who would one day put everything right.

Some prophets worked in northern kingdom of Israel (e.g., Elijah), others worked in southern kingdom of Judah (e.g., Isaiah). However, despite God's steadfast faithfulness, the people of Israel and Judah, as we have seen, would generally insist on going their own way. Of all the kings of Israel and Judah, only a few kings "did what was right in God's eye," as the biblical writers put it. Most of the kings led the people away from God rather than toward God.

When the northern kingdom of Israel was crushed and scattered by the Assyrians in 721 BC, God's people saw this as God's judgment on them for their sin. The southern kingdom of Judah held out for about another 150 years, but they too were crushed by an opponent, Babylonia, in 587 BC. Jerusalem was sacked. The glorious temple built by Solomon was destroyed, and the

Ark of the Covenant disappeared for all time. Thousands of Jews were exiled to Babylon.

Though the Persians defeated the Babylonians and allowed Jews to begin returning to Jerusalem in 538 BC, in many respects the exile never ended. Never again would Israel be free, led by a rightful king. By the time of Jesus, the Jews had been trading one oppressor for another, one pretender for another, for more than 500 years! The Jews knew that there was one God, who had created everything and who had chosen them from among all the peoples of the earth to be the ones through whom he would renew and restore his creation—it just didn't look like it. They wondered when they would be vindicated, when all the world would see that the Jews had been right. They prayed for God's kingdom to come.

Knowing the faithful and loving God

Given the vast expanse of the Old Testament, it is understandable that many Christians have trouble finding the God of love in its pages. Yet, if we learn to read the Old Testament better, we find story after story, poem after poem, about a faithful and loving God who pursues his faithless people, who made a promise to them and will not give it up. The story of Hosea is one of my favorites. It is a story about the love of God, from 700 years before Jesus.

The opening verses of Hosea certainly don't read like a love story. God tells Hosea that he is to go find an adulterous woman, marry her, and be a father to her children. Nothing about affection or courtship—just go and do it. The only

portion of the book that deals with Hosea's personal life is
1:2-10 and 3:1-5. Even here, the Hebrew is ambiguous and
scholars are all over the place on how best to translate it. Is
the woman, Gomer, a prostitute as some translations have it,
or is she "merely" promiscuous? Is she promiscuous before she
marries Hosea or only after? But if we keep in mind that we are
getting the story of two relationships in parallel, Hosea/Gomer
and YHWH/Israelites, then we can get the author's point.

Hosea is to enter into a marriage covenant with a woman who is
not faithful to the covenant, committing adultery with other men.
Similarly, God has entered into a covenant with the Israelites,
who have been unfaithful to that covenant by committing
adultery with foreign gods. The way Gomer's betrayal makes
Hosea feel is the way it makes God feel, but Hosea is to be
faithful to Gomer as God is faithful to Israel. This may not be
Hollywood's idea of a love story, but it is certainly God's.

Yes, the expected anger, judgment, and punishment await the
adulterous Israel (2:1-13); adultery has consequences. Yet, that
is not the end of the story. We are also told that God will win
Israel back by showering her with tender affection (2:14-23):
"Therefore I am now going to allure her; I will lead her into
the desert and speak tenderly to her. ... On that day, says the
Lord, you will call me 'My husband,' and no longer will you
call me 'My Baal'."

The same emotional playing out of betrayal, forgiveness, and
restoration is found in chapter 11: "How can I give you up,
Ephraim? How can I hand you over, O Israel? ... My heart
recoils within me; my compassion grows warm and tender,

I will not execute my fierce anger ... for I am God and no mortal, the Holy one in your midst, and I will not come in wrath." (11:8-9).

The overarching Old Testament story is that of covenant betrayal, judgment, and restoration. Nearly every Old Testament prophet comes bearing a word from God about the coming destruction of unfaithful Israel, but also brings a word of hope and restoration. The people will have to bear the consequences of their betrayal but God will one day restore them as his people, putting things right for them and for all of creation. It is this restoration (aka the coming of the kingdom of God) that the Jews are so anxiously awaiting in Jesus' day. It is the proclamation of God's kingdom, this restoration, which occupied much of Jesus' ministry and was accomplished in his death.

It isn't hard to see that this is somewhat like a marriage between a man and woman that has been rocked by unfaithfulness. It is hard and hurtful, marked by anger and despair. Yet, the couple makes it through, emerging on the other side with a marriage stronger than before. Is this really possible? With God, all things are possible.

True love

In *The Message*, Eugene Peterson writes, "Hosea is the prophet of love, but not love as we imagine or fantasize it. He was a parable of God's love for his people lived out as God revealed and enacted it—a lived parable. It is an astonishing story: a prophet commanded to marry a common whore and have children with her. It is an even more astonishing message: God loves us in just this way—goes after us at our worst, keeps after us until he gets us, and makes lovers of men and women who know nothing of real love. Once we absorb this story and the words that flow from it, we will know God far more accurately. And we will be well on our way to being cured of all the sentimentalized and neurotic distortions of love that incapacitate us from dealing with the God who loves us and loving the neighbors who don't love us."

Looking ahead

In the next chapter, we come to Act 4—the story of Jesus. God made a covenant with his people at Mount Sinai. Sadly, they weren't able to keep their end of the deal. Now, God steps in and provides a way for the covenant to be kept and thus usher in the arrival of God's kingdom.

A Bit More

The pagan gods

In this chapter's Scripture passages, there are references to Baal, Astarte, Milcom, Chemosh, and Molech.

These were various pagan gods worshipped by the peoples in the lands around the Israelites. Baal, for example, was the chief god of the Canaanites and is encountered often in the story of Israel.

The story of Israel was too often the story of God's people chasing after these false foreign gods and forgetting about the LORD God, the one true God, who had redeemed them from slavery in Egypt.

David

David is a towering figure in the story of God's people for several reasons. First, the Israelites came to embrace David as their greatest king, the man who consolidated the nation. For example, David conquered the city-state of Jerusalem, which was a neutral location belonging to none of the twelve tribes, and made it his capital. He brought the Ark of the Covenant to Jerusalem. His son, Solomon, would build God's temple there. Later, Solomon would take Israel to its zenith of military power and wealth, but Solomon also sowed the seeds of Israel's division into two kingdoms.

Second, David was more than just Israel's king. He was its poet, the composer of many psalms. The stories of David, Saul, Jonathan, Bathsheba, Absalom, and the rest are the most skillfully drawn narratives in the Old Testament. It is as if the writers and editors of the Hebrew Scriptures devoted their best and most poignant storytelling to the story of David, from his defeat of Goliath to his affair with Bathsheba to the tragedy of his son, Absalom.

But there is another reason that the Israelites and we are so drawn to the figure of David. He may have been Israel's greatest king and he may have been a "man after God's own heart," but David, like us all, made terrible and tragic mistakes. It is a little surprising that the writers of Samuel told the story of David and Bathsheba at all. The book of Chronicles leaves it out. In it we see the story of a powerful man who yielded to temptation, eventually arranging the murder of his pregnant lover's husband. Later, David would fail his own overambitious sons. Such stories reassure us that even David, anointed by God, could make terrible choices against God and others, and yet remain within God's loving, gracious grasp. This is Israel's story in the Old Testament—and our story too.

Why do Israel and Judah fall?

In the eighth century BC, the Assyrian empire posed an ever-growing threat to Israel and Judah. Lying to their northeast, this pressure was most acute on Israel. Nonetheless, Israel enjoyed peace and prosperity at times. One of these periods was from about 785-745 BC under King Jeroboam. Despite this period of peace and the complacency it brought, after Jeroboam's death the Assyrians overran the kingdom of Israel, wiping it from the map and exiling tens of thousands of the Israelites. The ten Israelite tribes that made up the northern kingdom would be "lost" forever, never again to be a national entity of any sort. These would be the lost tribes of Israel.

Why would this happen to Israel, and later, to Judah? We could leave God out of our explanation entirely, noting that Assyria and Babylonia were powerful and simply could not be stopped from their aggression. But this is not the biblical understanding. For the prophet Amos, Israel was no better or worse than its neighbors and that was precisely the problem. From Amos 3: "Hear this word that the Lord has spoken against you [Israel]. ... You only have I known of all the families of the earth; therefore I will punish you for your iniquities." Simply put, God expected more from his people. He held them to a higher standard, the standard of the covenant he had made with them. For Israel to be accused of oppressing the poor, as Amos accused them, was no small matter.

In failing to care for the needy while luxuriating in their own prosperity, Israel revealed the depth of its sin and the abandonment of its special relationship with YHWH, its Lord and God. Such abandonment could lead only to one outcome: destruction. The Israelites had forgotten that they were to care for the widow because God had cared for them. They had forgotten that they were to "let justice roll down like waters, and righteousness like an ever-flowing stream" (Amos 5:24). For the Jews, exile was a jail sentence for their many sins against God.

The promise keeper—Act 4

John 1:1-13 (NRSV)

In the beginning was the Word, and the Word was with God, and the Word was God. ² He was in the beginning with God. ³ All things came into being through him, and without him not one thing came into being. What has come into being ⁴ in him was life, and the life was the light of all people. ⁵ The light shines in the darkness, and the darkness did not overcome it.

⁶ There was a man sent from God, whose name was John. ⁷ He came as a witness to testify to the light, so that all might believe through him. ⁸ He himself was not the light, but he came to testify to the light. ⁹ The true light, which enlightens everyone, was coming into the world.

¹⁰ He was in the world, and the world came into being through him; yet the world did not know him. ¹¹ He came to what was his own, and his own people did not accept him. ¹² But to all who received him, who believed in his name, he gave power to become children of God, ¹³ who were born, not of blood or of the will of the flesh or of the will of man, but of God.

Romans 1:1-4, 16-17, 3:21-26 (NRSV)

Paul, a servant of Jesus Christ, called to be an apostle, set apart for the gospel of God, ² which he promised beforehand through his prophets in the holy scriptures, ³ the gospel concerning his Son, who was descended from David

according to the flesh ⁴ and was declared to be Son of God
with power according to the spirit of holiness by resurrection
from the dead, Jesus Christ our Lord, ...

¹⁶ For I am not ashamed of the gospel; it is the power of God
for salvation to everyone who has faith, to the Jew first and
also to the Greek. ¹⁷ For in it the righteousness of God is
revealed through faith for faith; as it is written, "The one
who is righteous will live by faith."

²¹ But now, apart from law, the righteousness of God has
been disclosed, and is attested by the law and the prophets,
²² the righteousness of God through faith in Jesus Christ[28] for
all who believe. For there is no distinction, ²³ since all have
sinned and fall short of the glory of God; ²⁴ they are now
justified by his grace as a gift, through the redemption that
is in Christ Jesus, ²⁵ whom God put forward as a sacrifice of
atonement by his blood, effective through faith. He did this
to show his righteousness, because in his divine forbearance
he had passed over the sins previously committed; ²⁶ it was
to prove at the present time that he himself is righteous and
that he justifies the one who has faith in Jesus.

*At the end of Act 3 all appeared lost. God's people had shown
themselves to be faithless countless times, unable to live up to their*

---

[28] or *through the faith of Jesus Christ*. This footnoted translation is now
dominant among North American Pauline scholars, including Kathryn
Grieb, Leander Keck, Richard Hays, and N. T. Wright. In 2011, it was
incorporated into the latest revision of the NIV. I've come to believe that
this "faith *of* Jesus Christ" translation is one of the keys to a truer and more
meaningful reading of Romans and the story of Christ.

end of the covenant with God. Did that mean God's promises would go forever unkept? Or would God find a new way?

Our story so far

In Acts 1 and 2, God creates everything, including humans in God's image. All is good until the humans rebel against God, seeking to be like gods themselves. This rebellion not only destroys the humans' relationship with God but damages God's creation. In Act 3, God sets out on a new course. The creator of the cosmos chooses one couple through whom all peoples would be blessed. God would save them and pursue them without end. God made a covenant to protect and preserve them, asking only two things in return, that they love God and love one another. But the people of God would remain rebellious and sinful, understanding little about what it really means to love.

So, when the curtain closes on Act 3 the question is this: Because God's people have proved unable to live up to their end of the covenant, would God's covenant promises of restoration and renewal go forever unkept?

When the curtain rises on Act 4, we find the story of a young Jewish maiden and the most extraordinary birth imaginable. We have come to the story of Jesus.

Approaching Jesus

Jesus was thoroughly and completely Jewish[29], born into first-century Judaism, with all its tensions and hopes. Much of Jesus' teachings and many of his actions only make sense in light of the beliefs and lives of first-century Jews. There are three keys to putting Jesus in the context of the biblical story.

First, we need to remember the purpose of the covenant God had made with his people. God had chosen Israel as the ones through whom all of creation would be renewed, salvation and peace would be brought to all, and God's kingdom would return to the earth. Thus, we should not be surprised that Jesus had more to say about the kingdom of God than any other subject. Jesus' healings were an enactment of God's kingdom, in which the blind would see and the oppressed would be set free. (See Luke 4:14-30, for Jesus' first public teachings and pronouncements about the arrival of God's kingdom.)

Second, if Israel was the God-chosen agent of creation's redemption, then the obvious question is *who* constitutes Israel. Israel was the nation of God's people—not a nation in the modern-day sense, but a people brought together under a covenant with God. God's people were those who worshipped

---

[29] It is sometimes hard for us to wrap our brains around this. Jesus was Jewish, as were all of his disciples, the apostle Paul, and all believers for at least ten years after Jesus' death and resurrection. The Jesus movement was a Jewish movement through and through. Indeed, Paul was even a Pharisee before he met Jesus on the road to Damascus (Acts 9). Paul considered himself a Jew until the day he died, one that had met and come to believe that Jesus was the long-awaited Jewish Messiah—and much more.

the Lord God, who kept the Sabbath, circumcised their male children, obeyed God's dietary laws, and so on. Keeping God's law was the badge of membership in the people of God.

Third, so the Jews, the people of God, believed in one God who had created all that is and had chosen them, the knowers and keepers of God's law. They believed that one day the whole world would see that they had been right and that they would be the ones through whom the world would be reconciled with God. However, it sure didn't look like it. By Jesus' day, the Jews had lived under foreign oppressors for more than 500 years. This is the driving tension in the Old Testament. Much of the story of Judaism in Jesus' day is the story of Jewish attempts to force God's hand, to try to make the fulfillment of all God's promises come true.

Act 4—The story of Jesus

The basics of Jesus' life can be told briefly and are agreed upon by all but the most skeptical of historians:

> In about 6 BC[30], a young Jewish woman gave birth to a baby and named him Jesus. When this Jesus was around 30, he began a public ministry of teaching, proclaiming, and miracle-doing. Jesus' growing confrontation with the Jewish

---

[30] Don't be thrown off by this. Though our calendars were built with Jesus' birth at AD 1, the calendar makers got some things wrong. We know that Herod the Great, who ordered the Bethlehem massacre of infant boys, died in 4BC. Hence, Jesus had to be born before that.

leadership culminated in his crucifixion by the
Roman governor, Pontius Pilate, in about AD
30. After his death, some of Jesus' followers
claimed that he had been resurrected.

That seems a pretty sparse telling, but the bare facts, about
which nearly all people—believer and non-believer alike—
agree, are pretty simple. But what did it all mean? Did Jesus die
a tragic figure, a failed would-be Messiah? Or was Jesus truly
resurrected? And if so, what would that mean?

Each of the four gospels provides an interpretation of the story
of Jesus. They are four portraits of one Jesus. Likewise, the
rest of the New Testament provides additional interpretation
of Jesus, both the person and the event. Proclaiming that, yes,
Jesus was actually resurrected by God, the New Testament
writers explore the meaning and implications of this, for the
world and for each of us.

If Act 3 in our play is the story of a tragedy, that of a people
unable to simply love God and one another, than what is Act
4? Let's take a look at the Christian answer to this question.

The meaning of Jesus?

Why was Jesus born? For what purpose? Why did God humble
himself, taking on a full-blooded humanity? If your answer to
these questions is "to save us," you are right so far as it goes. But
God's rescue involves far more than just us. It is the keeping of
promises that God made long before, way back at the beginning

of Act 3. Seeing Jesus as a promise kept is essential to grasping the biblical story. Here's how it works.

Jesus and Paul lived in a time of great turmoil, as many Jews resisted Roman rule. They remembered God's extravagant promises and awaited the day when God would finally keep his promises, when, as written in the scroll of Jeremiah, "I [God] will cause a righteous Branch to spring up for David; and he shall execute justice and righteousness in the land."

But they had waited a long time, and it was natural for some to wonder if God's promises would forever go unfulfilled. The Jews knew they weren't keeping up their end of the bargain— that they really love God and neighbor every day.

Yet, *God had made the promise.* And, for Paul, God is righteous and keeps the promises he makes. He came to see that in Jesus, God had kept those promises—through the faithfulness of Jesus to God and to the vocation given to him by God. Jesus was the way out of the covenant dilemma. In a sense, Jesus was the "righteousness of God" in the flesh. Despite the unwillingness or inability of the Jews to live up to the covenant and to be the light to the world, God had provided the means of covenant-keeping. This means was Jesus Christ, the one Jew who did truly love God and love neighbor without fail. Jesus' own faithfulness to the covenant all the way to a Roman cross revealed that God is not only the promise maker, but the promise keeper. In Christ, God's covenant people had been restored to a right relationship with God. Hence, they had been saved. And who are these covenant people? Namely those who have faith in Jesus Christ who is, in essence, their representative Messiah, making Jesus' faithfulness their own faithfulness.

To say this another way, God's righteousness (his covenant faithfulness) was revealed to the world through the faithfulness of Jesus Christ, for the rescuing of all who believe. Christians' claim is this: God's saving justice, his covenant faithfulness, was unveiled in the person of Jesus Christ.

But a crucified Messiah?

Because we believe that Jesus was the Jewish Messiah and was also crucified, it is hard for us to grasp that for any first-century Jew, *crucified Messiah* was an oxymoron, i.e., a combination of contradictory words. So far as the Jews were concerned, there was simply no way that God's Messiah could end up on a Roman cross. Such an idea was absurd, foolish, crazy. The fact that Jesus ended up dead on a cross could mean only one thing—that he wasn't the Messiah, that once again the hopes of Israel had been dashed upon the rocks of Roman reality. On that dark Friday afternoon, anything that we might call a "Jesus movement" collapsed. The disciples went into hiding, fearful that they too would be picked up by the Jewish leadership or the Romans.

But when Jesus is raised to newly embodied life by God, it is the *proof* that although Jesus was crucified by the Romans, he was nonetheless God's Messiah. It is the resurrection that turned the phrase *crucified Messiah* from an absurdity into a revelation of God's love and faithfulness.

We shouldn't be surprised that the apostles met so much resistance as they worked to carry this good news.[31] As Paul put it, "we proclaim Messiah crucified, a stumbling block to Jews and foolishness to Greeks [meaning simply, non-Jews]" (1 Cor.1:23).

The resurrection[32] of Jesus was his vindication, the proof that he was right all along and that the salvation of Israel and hence the whole world had been won through his journey of suffering, shame, and death. The resurrection is the reason why there are Christians at all. Had Jesus' death been the end of the story, there would be no Christians, no teachings preserved, no stories told.

Yet, for all that, the resurrection is not the climax of the story; it was not the place of God's victory over sin and death. That

---

[31] The Gospel of Mark was the first gospel written. In Mark, the first words by Jesus are, "The time is fulfilled, and the kingdom of God has come near; repent, and believe in the good news" (Mark 1:15). Any first-century Jew would have heard these words as a proclamation that the story of God's people was coming to a climax. In the Greek, "good news" or "gospel" is *evangelion*. This was not a "church word." Instead, the *evangelion* was a proclamation that a new emperor had been borne, had taken the throne, or won an important military victory. This proclamation was carried to the Roman provinces by heralds, or messengers. The good news, or *evangelion*, that Jesus brings is the claim that Jesus is Lord, not Caesar or anyone else. This proclamation, that all other claims to lordship are false, set Jesus up in direct competition with Caesar and those who would deny that "the kingdom of God has come near."

[32] There is much to say about resurrection and much "unlearning" to do, but that will come in the second part of this book, when we take a closer at the most basic Christian beliefs.

place was the cross. Here again is Paul: "For the message of the cross is foolishness to those who are perishing, but to us who are being the saved it is the power of God" (1 Cor. 1:18).

The Good in Good Friday

But how could that be? How could God's victory be won via Jesus' death? How could it be that our reconciliation with God is accomplished on that cross?

These questions swirl around the word "atonement." You can think of it as "at-one-ment," putting us "at-one" with God, i.e., putting our relationship right. It is a relational idea and speaks to our relationship to God.

Though the New Testament writers are clear that this atonement has been accomplished via the cross, they do not offer any single theory of how it works. Instead, we get various images. For example, one image is grounded in the courtroom: Jesus stands in our place and takes the punishment that is our due. Another image is taken from the slave market: God redeems us from our bondage. Yet another image is that of a pardon, taken from the language of kings. None of these images tell the whole story by themselves; together, they provide a rich picture of how it is that Jesus put us right with God.

Putting it all together

Here is a way to tell the story that I think is faithful to the biblical writings and puts the credit for our salvation where it belongs, not on us but upon God:

God made a promise to Abraham that the world would be put right and that it would be done through his own family—indeed, that all the families of the earth would be blessed through them. God rescued Abraham's family from slavery in Egypt, making a covenant with them, teaching them how to live in right relationship with God and one another. He would be their God, they would be his people, and one day the world would be put right; justice and mercy would remake the planet.

God's teaching boiled down to two things: love God and love neighbor. Yet, tragically, this love-filled life proved impossible for God's people. They chased after other gods, and they failed to love their neighbors every day. They even lost sight of who their neighbors were. They forgot that all the families of the earth were to be blessed through them. They imagined that they had some sort of exclusive claim on God.

It became sadly evident that God's promise to restore and renew the cosmos could not be kept, for his people could not keep their end of the bargain. So what did that mean, would God's promise stay unfulfilled forever?

In a word, no. God would provide one Jew who would be utterly faithful to the covenant, loving God and loving neighbor every day and in every way. God, in the person of Jesus, would do and be for Israel what Israel was unable to do and be for herself.

Of course, such love put Jesus on a collision course with the powers of this world, who had long forgotten God's ways. Jesus' path would take him to that cross. It had to, for the only way off that path was for Jesus to abandon the vocation given him by God. But, instead, Jesus was faithful all the way to the cross. The covenant had been kept by this one faithful Jew, and the restored relationship of this kept covenant can be ours, if we only trust Jesus and embrace him as our representative Messiah, the one whose faithfulness revealed that God is not only the great promise-maker but the great promise-keeper.

And how do we know that this is a true story? Because God raised Jesus to new life and gave him dominion over the heavens and the earth. Alleluia!

In the next chapter, we go on to Act 5. This is the act in which you and I live; we are part of the story. God forms the believers into a church, empowering them to be the light to the world and to make disciples. It is time for all the world to come to the Lord God!

Our Place in God's Story—Act 5

Acts 2:1-4 (NIV)

When the day of Pentecost came, they were all together in one place. [2] Suddenly a sound like the blowing of a violent wind came from heaven and filled the whole house where they were sitting. [3] They saw what seemed to be tongues of fire that separated and came to rest on each of them. [4] All of them were filled with the Holy Spirit and began to speak in other tongues as the Spirit enabled them.

1 Peter 2:4-5, 9-10 (NIV)

[4] As you come to him, the living Stone—rejected by humans but chosen by God and precious to him—[5] you also, like living stones, are being built into a spiritual house to be a holy priesthood, offering spiritual sacrifices acceptable to God through Jesus Christ.

[9] But you are a chosen people, a royal priesthood, a holy nation, God's special possession, that you may declare the praises of him who called you out of darkness into his wonderful light. [10] Once you were not a people, but now you are the people of God; once you had not received mercy, but now you have received mercy.

Romans 12:9-18 (NIV)

[9] Love must be sincere. Hate what is evil; cling to what is good. [10] Be devoted to one another in love. Honor one another above yourselves. [11] Never be lacking in zeal, but keep your spiritual fervor, serving the Lord. [12] Be joyful in hope, patient in affliction, faithful in prayer. [13] Share with the Lord's people who are in need. Practice hospitality.

[14] Bless those who persecute you; bless and do not curse. [15] Rejoice with those who rejoice; mourn with those who mourn. [16] Live in harmony with one another. Do not be proud, but be willing to associate with people of low position. Do not be conceited.

[17] Do not repay anyone evil for evil. Be careful to do what is right in the eyes of everyone. [18] If it is possible, as far as it depends on you, live at peace with everyone.

What could possibly follow Act 4, the story of Jesus' life, death, and resurrection? Where could the story go? The truth is that it comes to us. It is the story of God's Spirit forming God's people into the church and empowering them to build for the kingdom of God.

We are fast approaching the end of our six-act play, this telling of the entire biblical story from Genesis to Revelation, from the beginning to the end. In this chapter, we come to Act 5, the story of the church, the body of Christ. It is in the midst of this act that we find ourselves.

Let's begin again by looking again at the story to this point. In Acts 1 and 2, God creates everything, including humans, in

God's image. All is good until the humans rebel against God, destroying the humans' relationship with God and distorting God's good creation. In Act 3, God forms a people through whom all would be put right. He makes a covenant with them and pursues them relentless, even as they insist on going their own way. When it becomes clear that this people, the Israelites, are unable simply to love God and neighbor, it looks as if the project of renewal and restoration might forever languish.

But in Act 4, God provides the one faithful Jew, his own son, who would truly love God and neighbor, who would keep the covenant. Thus, through the faith of Jesus Christ, the representative Messiah, the people of God are restored to a right relationship with God, whose victory over sin and death was won on a cross and through whom the kingdom of God had arrived.

When the curtain falls on Act 4, we can rightly ask: *What's next?* If Jesus ushered in the kingdom of God, what could Act 5 be about? This is really our own question. What are we about? What is our own place in God's story?

The answer to these questions is the story of Act 5. It is yet unfinished, and we are part of it every day. It is the story of God's church, the fellowship formed by and empowered by God's Holy Spirit. And the story begins at the Jewish festival of Pentecost, six weeks after Jesus' crucifixion and resurrection.

The Holy Spirit returns

When Acts 5 opens, Jesus' disciples have gathered in Jerusalem for the Festival of Pentecost. The city is packed, with the population having swelled to more than 150,000 people. Jews are there from all over the Roman Empire. In the weeks before the festival, the disciples had been with the resurrected Jesus, who, before returning to the Father, told them that they were to remain in Jerusalem to wait for the promised arrival of the Holy Spirit. Jesus had explained that God's Spirit would come upon them with power so that they could be Jesus' witnesses in Jerusalem, Judea, Samaria, and "to the ends of the earth" (see Acts 1).

One can only imagine the anticipation and, perhaps, anxiety that the disciples felt. Only weeks before, they had been cowering in an upstairs room waiting to be rounded up by the Roman soldiers after Jesus' crucifixion. But Jesus had passed through death to newly embodied life; his resurrection had changed everything. They didn't know what to expect, but they wouldn't have to wait long to find out what was in store for them. As Luke tells it, they were gathered together when "from heaven there came a sound like the rush of a violent wind. … Divided tongues, as of fire … rested on each of them. All of them were filled with the Holy Spirit and began to speak in other languages." As Jesus had promised, the Holy Spirit had returned with power. *Returned?*

Ever since the flight from Egypt more than a millennium before Christ, God had been present with his people in a way that he was not present elsewhere. Indeed, God's dwelling place had been the temple in Jerusalem. But God's people had been unable to live as they should in the presence of God. Consequently, God's presence had departed the temple: "Then the glory of the Lord went out from the threshold of the house ..." (Ezekiel 10:18). Although he would no longer dwell with them as he had, God had not forever abandoned his people. God promised that one day he would put within them a new spirit, replacing their hearts of stone with hearts of flesh (see Jeremiah 31). Now, as the disciples sat together, that day had come, the Holy Spirit had returned.

What does it mean?

When the Holy Spirit came upon the disciples, they were able to speak in languages that they couldn't possibly have known. It would be like me leaping up and speaking in Russian. The disciples weren't speaking nonsense. They were speaking languages that could be understood by festival pilgrims from all over the empire. It was as if God was undoing the scattering of languages that followed his destruction of the Tower of Babel (Genesis 11).

Needless to say, the crowds were "amazed and perplexed." What was going on? What could such a thing possibly mean? Some in the crowd tried to dismiss the whole spectacle, accusing the disciples of drunkenness. But the disciples were not drunk and Peter rose to explain to the crowds what was happening.

"The disciples are not drunk," Peter said. "This is God's work! Prophecies are being fulfilled. The kingdom of God is at hand. Through Jesus' life, death, and resurrection, it is all happening."

This is not alcohol talking, but the Holy Spirit, who is the sign of Christ's power and glory and who is empowering the disciples to do the work of the kingdom. Rather than trying to dismiss the disciples' miraculous abilities, Peter tells them, the crowds ought to repent so that their sins will be forgiven and they too will receive the gift of the Holy Spirit. And so it begins ...

God builds his church

The Book of Acts is the second half of a two-volume work by Luke. In it, he tells the story of the 30 years or so after Jesus' death and resurrection. An important key to understanding Acts is to see that the driver in the story, the one who makes things happen, is the Holy Spirit. From the story of Pentecost, Luke goes on to tell us about the establishment and growth of the church in Jerusalem and how Jewish leaders began their attempts to stamp out this blasphemous cult.

Three or so years after Jesus' resurrection, one of these, the Pharisee Saul, was visited by the living Christ while on his way to round up Christians in Damascus (Acts 9). Saul, now called Paul, emerges as a leader in the early church and becomes the missionary to the Gentiles. Acts tells us of three missionary journeys Paul made over a period of eight or so years (AD 50-58): one trip in Asia Minor and two trips through Greece. Many of Paul's letters in the New Testament were written to churches he founded on these trips: 1 & 2 Corinthians, 1 & 2 Thessalonians, Philippians, and so on. The Book of Acts closes with Paul in Rome under house arrest as he awaits trial before Caesar. This was probably about AD 62.

With the exception of most of Paul's letters and, perhaps, Mark's gospel, all the New Testament writings are from the three decades after the end of Acts. They tell the story of the church striving to stay true to God's teachings in a hostile world.

We'll talk more about the Holy Spirit in the second part of this book, but for now, I want to consider what sort of church we are to be. Are we to be a church with the passion demonstrated by Peter on Pentecost?

Something big

Read through any company's annual reports and you'll find a common theme. Every year is "momentous" and "without precedent." Every year, according to the reports, management is faced with difficulties and challenges that have never been seen before. Listen to politicians and pundits. Even theologians and teachers. It seems that we always want to believe that we live in momentous times, perhaps the most important period in our nation's, or company's, or church's history. Why? Why is it so important for us to believe we face challenges greater than anyone has faced before us?

It is because we all want to be part of something big. We want to be part of something that transcends the ordinariness of our daily lives. We need to believe that our lives and our work *really* matter. Thus, it is all the more odd that many Christians so easily marginalize "church." Church becomes a place to see friends for a little while on Sunday morning, or a place where we come to learn a little more about how to be nice or how to be happy, but certainly nothing BIG.

In the second of this chapter's Scripture passages, Peter blows out of the water all attempts to marginalize church and faith. Christians, he writes, are a community chosen and formed by God so that we might proclaim God to the world, so that all those who are blind to God's "mighty acts" might see the truth. Re-read the passage from 1 Peter. Peter's words ought to make your heart race a bit, stoking passion there. God desires for us to be passionate disciples *so that* we might be a passionate church *so that* we may effectively proclaim God to the world in what we say and what we do—in who we are. Peter wrote to encourage Christians who were being persecuted and shunned. He sought to strengthen their resolve by reminding them of their true identities. They were the people of God, God's colonists as it were, who would never be abandoned by God and whose purpose could never be diminished. We are no less the people of God, chosen for a purpose larger than ourselves.

What's a passionate church look like?

Like Peter, Paul wanted to help the newly formed Christian communities grasp their true identity. Also like Peter, Paul would go on to teach these communities what it meant to live as God's people. This was not about showing the Christians how to be happy or even nice. All of Paul's teachings about Christian behavior can be summed up this way: do what builds up the community, do what is a good witness to those on the outside, avoid what tears down the community, and avoid what is a bad witness. For Paul, contributing to the needs of others and showing hospitality (v. 13 in this chapter's passage from Romans) are good acts in themselves, but they are part of the larger purpose. Generosity and kindness proclaim to others God's goodness and power.

I want to be clear here. Living in harmony with one another (v. 16), rejoicing with those who rejoice, weeping with those who weep (v. 15)—these are all good in and of themselves. But they are part of a larger purpose. Loving one another with mutual affection (v. 10) is part of how we carry out God's charge to us to be the light to the world. God calls us to love God and one another *with passion*, to build up our churches *with passion*, to protect the community that God has entrusted to us with *passion*, to serve others *with passion*, to give *with passion*, to learn *with passion*. Always and everything, *with passion*. Notice what Paul writes in v. 11: "Do not lag in zeal, be ardent in spirit, serve the Lord." Paul is talking here about what we've been calling passion. Are we passionate about Jesus? Are we a passionate church? Here is how Eugene Peterson has rendered v. 10 in *The Message*: "Don't burn out: keep yourselves fueled and aflame." Do our hearts burn? They should.

Looking ahead

Stories have endings. God's story, too, is heading somewhere, toward the complete restoration of all God's creation. Yet, the ending is not like others. The end is not an event, to be found on a timeline. At the end is a person, the Alpha and Omega, the Lord God Almighty, the beginning and the end. The final act in God's drama is the story of the end.

A Bit More

Who are the people of God?

Who are the people of God? Who will spend eternity in loving communion with God? Who will see God's face (Rev 22:4)? The Jews of Jesus' day rightly understood that they had been chosen by God to be his agents in the renewal of all creation—the Jews were God's people. But … who was a Jew? The people of God were those who lived in covenant relationship with God and submitted themselves to the obligations of that covenant. If you worshipped the Lord God and strived to keep his Law, you were a Jew; you were part of God's people. Ruth was not an Israelite, but because she chose to follow the Lord God and keep his law, she became part of God's people and was the great-grandmother of King David. When the Jews understood this correctly (they sometimes forgot), they knew that "Jewish-ness" was not a matter of DNA, but of keeping God's law.

Thus, we should not be surprised that many of the first Christians, all of whom were Jewish, believed that one had to become a Jew first, in order to become a Christian. Some early Christians, like Paul, disagreed. In practice, this became an argument over circumcision. For many Jewish Christians, including Peter, the circumcision of male children was a sign of God's covenant, and if a male gentile wanted to become part of God's people, he had to be circumcised.

Paul saw this very differently. He argued that because of Jesus, the "badge of membership" in the people of God had changed. No longer were God's people marked out by their keeping of the Law, but by their faith in Jesus Christ. If a Jewish Christian wanted to keep the law, that was fine; but it was not required. The only "marker" of God's people was to be faith in Jesus Christ. If you placed your trust in Jesus, you were part of God's people; if you did not place your trust in Jesus, you were not part of God's people. In about AD 50, this debate was settled in the Christian community at a council in Jerusalem (Acts 15). The council affirmed the admission of gentiles (non-Jews) into the church without any requirement of circumcision.

This can all get terribly confusing if you do not remember that ALL the first Christians were Jews. It was ten years or so after Jesus' resurrection before a non-Jew became a Christian. Most Jews did not become Christians. They did not accept Jesus as Messiah, much less as God himself. It is not hard to see why. Jews in Jesus' day awaited a Messiah who would come in power and might and wonder and glory. To them, the idea that the Messiah would end up crucified on a Roman cross was absurd. Indeed, in their mind, any "would-be" Messiah who got himself crucified was, quite obviously, not the Messiah after all.

The End of Tears—Act 6

Revelation 19:6-8 (NRSV)

[6]Then I heard what seemed to be the voice of a great multitude, like the sound of many waters and like the sound of mighty thunderpeals, crying out,

"Hallelujah!
For the Lord our God
the Almighty reigns.
[7]Let us rejoice and exult
and give him the glory,
for the marriage of the Lamb has come,
and his bride has made herself ready;
[8]to her it has been granted to be clothed
with fine linen, bright and pure"—
for the fine linen is the righteous deeds of the saints.

Revelation 21:1-6 (NRSV)

Then I saw a new heaven and a new earth; for the first heaven and the first earth had passed away, and the sea was no more. [2]And I saw the holy city, the new Jerusalem, coming down out of heaven from God, prepared as a bride adorned for her husband. [3]And I heard a loud voice from the throne saying,

"See, the home of God is among mortals.
He will dwell with them as their God;
they will be his peoples,
and God himself will be with them;

⁴he will wipe every tear from their eyes.

Death will be no more;

mourning and crying and pain will be no more,

for the first things have passed away."

⁵And the one who was seated on the throne said, "See, I am making all things new." Also he said, "Write this, for these words are trustworthy and true." ⁶Then he said to me, "It is done! I am the Alpha and the Omega, the beginning and the end. To the thirsty I will give water as a gift from the spring of the water of life."

We started "in the beginning" and now we come to "the End." But this End is not an event or a time, but a person: our Lord, indeed the Lord of all, Jesus Christ.

We have arrived at the end of our journey through the entire biblical story. Thus, we have come to Act 6 in our six-act play. This is the story of Jesus' return and the renewal of all of God's creation. It is the final consummation of all that God had promised to Abraham, to Moses, and to all the prophets of old. It is where God's work has always been headed.

For the last time, let's take a brief look at the whole story to this point.[33] In Act 1, God creates everything, makes the humans in his image. All is good. But Act 2 tells the story of

---

[33] If it seems a bit repetitive to go back through the story again, that is because I am intending to be repetitive, albeit in different words. As disciples of Jesus, we need to absorb this story, breathing it in so that this story of God's saving work can reshape the lens through which we see the world and the hearts with which we love.

human rebellion and God's determination to put right what the humans have wrecked. In Act 3, God chooses one couple, Abraham and Sarah, through whose family all the families of the earth would be blessed. God also makes a promise to protect and preserve this family, his people. But this promise is a covenant, a two-way agreement. For their part, the people of God are to love God and one another. However, instead they would remain rebellious and sinful, understanding little about what it really means to love. Sadly, God's people proved unable to live up to their end of the agreement. It seems that God's purposes will be thwarted by human stubbornness.

But, of course, God's purposes must move forward. When God makes a promise, God keeps that promise. Thus, in Act 4, we learn that God provided, in his only Son, the one faithful Jew who would truly love God and neighbor, who would keep the people's covenant with God. Through the faith of Jesus Christ, this representative Messiah, the people of God are restored to a right relationship with God and the kingdom of God is ushered in.

Of course, anyone can look around and see that tragedy and grief and poverty and illness are still with us. It is as if God's kingdom has come already … but not yet.[34] There is still work to do. This is the story of Act 5, our own place in the larger story. Act 5 is yet unfinished, and we are part of it every day. It is the story of God's Church, the fellowship formed by and

---

[34] Take a few minutes and read the supplemental reading at the end of this chapter. I think it will help.

empowered by God's Holy Spirit. It is the work of making disciples and building for the kingdom of God.

But when will this work be complete? When will God's saving purposes be consummated? When will the kingdom of God be a present reality to all? This is the story of Act 6.

Jesus returns, the Bridegroom comes to his bride

Marriage as a metaphor for God's relationship with his people is one of the most enduring and profound of all biblical images. The power of the metaphor is grounded in the significance of covenant. The marriage of a man and a woman is a covenant, instituted by God, to which both are expected to remain faithful. Not surprisingly then, Jesus is repeatedly referred to as the Bridegroom. John the Baptist is a friend of the groom (John 3:22-30). When Jesus is asked by the Pharisees why his disciples don't fast, he tells them that the disciples are wedding guests who won't fast while they are with the groom (Mark 2:18-22). Numerous parables liken Jesus' ministry and the coming kingdom of God to a wedding feast.

All this prepares us for the images in John's vision in the Book of Revelation, on which I will elaborate simply because so many people are put off by Revelation.

We are nearing the end of the story. The Lamb, Christ, is almost ready for his marriage to his bride, the church. Jesus' second coming will be the consummation of this marriage. In Revelation 19, an angel arrives, bearing a message of salvation: "Blessed are those who are invited to the marriage supper of the

Lamb," recalling Jesus' parable of a wedding feast that focuses on invitations rejected and accepted (Matthew 22:1-14). There are other places in the New Testament that refer to Jesus' second coming, but this marriage supper from John's visions is the most poetic. How else would one really talk about the Lord's return and the restoration of all things? This image of the marriage supper is meant to convey to us that the consummation of all God's work, the entire rescue project, has come.

It is important to grasp that the Lamb and his bride are married not only in the future, but in the present. We often make the mistake of thinking of time as only linear. But we live post-Einstein. According to his theories, which have been borne out, time passes more slowly for an astronaut circling the earth at high speed than it does for us on the ground, relative to one another. The astronaut's "after" is my "before." If the astronaut's "before" and my "before" aren't the same, why should I assume that "before" and "after" have any fixed meaning with God?

We struggle to make sense of the New Testament's perspective that God's kingdom has come already, but not yet. We struggle to grasp that the people of God are not just waiting to be the bride, but are already the bride. In the glorious images of Revelation 21, God comes to dwell with his people. And yet God dwells already with his people. We are God's temple. The Holy Spirit is God dwelling amongst us. All this takes a massive feat of imagination, and Revelation is written for the imagination. John's visions are meant to help us imagine the truth of a reality larger than we see and touch in our daily lives.

God wins

Though the details of the story may be difficult for us to grasp, when we get out of those details, the story becomes clear. God wins. Satan loses. Jesus reigns. And at the very end of all this, just before the arrival of the "new heaven and new earth" (Rev. 21:1), all the dead are resurrected. On this point, there is much support in the New Testament. Just as Jesus was raised, so shall we all be raised. We affirm this when we recite the Apostles' Creed and its promise of the "resurrection of the body." More on that in Part 2.

It is important to grasp that across the entire Bible, Old Testament and New, this resurrection is of *all* people, those who have come to God and those who have not. All people.

And then all people, now resurrected, stand to be judged, each "according to what they had done" (Rev. 20:13). All this is recorded in a book, what we might call the book of merit. I don't know about you, but many of my entries in this book deserve God's condemnation.

Blessedly, however, there is a second book, the "Book of Life" (Rev. 20:12). And all those whose names are found in that book go on to eternity with God and one another in the "new heaven and new earth." Of course, in whom is there life? In the Father, the Son, and the Holy Spirit. Jesus is, as he claimed, the "resurrection and the life" (John 11:25). We are made right with God by trusting in Jesus, in his rescue of us. This is the New Testament through and through. Those whose names are written in the Book of Life are marked by their faith in Christ.

A new heaven and a new earth

With all the dead resurrected and all the faithful moving on to eternity with Christ, Revelation's final visions in chapters 21 and 22 paint stunning images of the fulfillment of God's promises. After all went so tragically wrong in the Garden, God came to Abraham and Sarah and promised to put things right through them, so that all the families of the earth would be blessed through them (Genesis 12:3). Now, in Revelation 22, the leaves of the tree of life (the tree from the Garden of Eden story) are for "the healing of the nations."

Moses could not see the face of God and live (Exodus 33:12-23) but here in Revelation 22, we are told that God's people "will see his face and his name will be on their forehead."

The prophets looked ahead to an enormous burst of God's creativity with the arrival of a new heaven and new earth (Isaiah 65:17). Now in Revelation 21:1, they arrive; heaven comes to earth. Or to put it better, earth and heaven become one.

Every hope, every dream that lies in our hearts come to their realization in these last two chapters. Reconciliation, hope, health, peace, joy, and life itself. They are all here in the abundance of God's grace.

And as with the rest of Revelation, the closing visions are like a stained glass window in which each fragment of glass is borrowed from earlier in the story that began with Genesis. The "new heaven and new earth" is from Isaiah 65 and 66. The loud voices from the throne sing from Ezekiel, as well as Isaiah 35 and 65. The water of life evokes for us the story of Jesus and the Samaritan woman at the well to whom he promises "a spring of water that gushes up to eternal life" (John 4). There is the tree of life, which we have not seen since Genesis 3 when the humans were exiled from the Garden of Eden, denying them access to this tree that gives eternal life.

Of course, much of this can be hard to see. The library of sacred writings we call the Bible is vast. It's easy to get lost in its expanse. 66 books. 1,189 chapters. 31,102 verses[35]. Written, compiled, and edited over many centuries. Millennia ago. Yet, there is an overarching narrative to this vast library. Here is the story, told not in six acts, but in 109 words:

> God created the cosmos, pronounced it good, and made humans in his image. He gave them a beautiful place to live and work. Yet, tragically, they tossed it all away for the chance to be like gods themselves. So God set about to put things right. God chose a people, Abraham and his descendants, through whom this restoration would proceed. In the end, God, in the person of Jesus Christ, did for Israel and all humanity what they were and we still are unable to do for ourselves—simply to love God and to love

---

[35] No need to e-mail me if you have a different number. It all depends on which translation is used, the underlying Hebrew and Greek texts, and who is doing the counting. It is helpful to remember that the original texts had no chapter and verse divisions; these were added much later.

neighbor, enabling the rescue of God's people
and the restoration of God's good creation.

It is this restoration of God's creation that is depicted at the
end of Revelation with the arrival of the new heaven and new
earth.

The Holy City comes to us

One of the things that should surprise you the most about
Revelation is that the Holy City, the New Jerusalem, comes
to earth, not vice versa. The story doesn't end with God's
people being spirited way to some distant spot in the cosmos,
but with heaven coming to earth. I am pretty sure this is not
how many Christians envision eternity. Don't we head off to
spend eternity in our true home, the "place" we came from?
No. This is Plato creeping into things. In Revelation, the City
of God, the New Jerusalem, the Holy City comes here! The
city comes down out of heaven (21:10). N. T. Wright [36] helps
us to grasp this crucial aspect of John's vision:

> Heaven and earth, it seems, are not after all poles
> apart, needing to be separated forever when
> all the children of heaven have been rescued
> from this wicked earth. Nor are they simply
> different ways of looking at the same thing, as
> would be implied by some kinds of pantheism.
> No: they are different, radically different; but

---

[36] Wright, N. T. (2007). *Surprised by Hope* (116-117). London: Society for
Promoting Christian Knowledge.

they are made for each other in the same way (Revelation is suggesting) as male and female. And, when they finally come together, that will be cause for rejoicing in the same way that a wedding is: a creational sign that God's project is going forward; that opposite poles within creation are made for union, not competition; that love and not hate have the last word in the universe; and that fruitfulness and not sterility is God's will for creation.

What is promised in this passage, then, is what Isaiah foresaw: a new heaven and a new earth, replacing the old heaven and the old earth, which were bound to decay. This doesn't mean, as I have stressed throughout, that God will wipe the slate clean and start again. If that were so, there would be no celebration, no conquest of death, no long preparation now at last complete. As the chapter develops, the Bride, the wife of the Lamb, is described lovingly: she is the New Jerusalem promised by the prophets of the exile, especially Ezekiel.

But, unlike in Ezekiel's vision, where the rebuilt Temple takes eventual center stage, there is no Temple in this city (21:22). The Temple in Jerusalem was always designed, it seems, as a pointer to, and an advance symbol for, the presence of God himself. When the reality is there, the signpost is no longer necessary. As in Romans and 1 Corinthians, the living God will dwell with and among his people, filling the city with his life and love, and pouring out grace and healing in the river of life that flows from the city out to the nations.

There is a sign here of the future project that awaits the redeemed, in God's eventual new world. So far from sitting on clouds playing harps, as people often imagine, the redeemed people of God in the new world will be the agents of his love going out in new ways, to accomplish new creative tasks, to celebrate and extend the glory of his love.

The end is a who

I suppose we can't help but think of Revelation's conclusion as The End, in particular, the end of our play, like the final credits that roll at the end of a movie. Certainly, the Bible helps us to grasp God's story and our place in it. As Wright puts it, we are the ones in the story between Acts and Revelation. And, yes, one of the many gifts of the Jews to us all, as Tom Cahill[37] put it, is the knowledge that we are headed somewhere, that history has an arc, a destination.

But we should never forget that at The End, stands not an event or even a place, as wonderfully as that place might be

---

[37] Tom Cahill's book, *The Gift of the Jews*, is excellent though a bit rough in places. Then again, the ancient world was often a very rough place.

depicted in John's visions. Standing there is a person, the Lamb, Jesus the Christ. He is the beginning and the end, the Alpha and the Omega. He is the substance of our hopes and the embodiment of God's promises. However wonderful I might imagine eternity with Christ to be, I am imagining in black-and-white, compared to the glories of God's colors. As hope-crushing as our present sufferings may be, the light of Christ, a light that shines with the brilliance of a thousand suns, beckons us and those we love to join him, now and forever.

Maranatha … Come, Lord Jesus, Come (Revelation 22:20)

A Bit More

The already/not yet perspective

I don't think there is anything more important to reading the New Testament well and, at the same time, more difficult to teach than the reality that the kingdom of God has come *already, but not yet*. This perspective permeates the New Testament from beginning to end and can be quickly seen in something as mundane as verb tenses. Gordon Fee[38] writes:

---

[38] Gordon D. Fee, *Paul, the Spirit, and the People of God* (Peabody, Mass.: Hendrickson Publishers, 1996), 52.

For Paul, therefore, God's final salvation of his people has already been accomplished by Christ. In a sort of divine time warp, the future condemnation we all richly deserve has been transferred from the future into the past, having been borne by Christ (Rom. 8:1-3). Thus, we "have been saved" (Eph. 2:8). Since our final salvation has not been fully realized, he can likewise speak of salvation as something presently in process "we are being saved," (1 Cor. 1:18) and as yet to be completed ("we shall be saved," Rom 5:9). Redemption is both "already" (Eph. 1:7) and "not yet" (Eph. 4:30), as is our "adoption" (Rom 8:15 and 23) and "justification" (Rom 5:1; Gal. 5:5).

I invite you to check out these verses and others. Is Paul merely confused about his grammar? Hardly! He is working out the implications of Jesus' resurrection and the coming of God's kingdom. (Resurrection is part of the larger package called the kingdom of God.) What does it mean for a world still wracked with sin and tragedy? Did Jesus get the job only partly done? No. I hope the following explanation will be helpful.

Jesus the Messiah

Jesus proclaimed the fulfillment of the Jewish hope and demonstrated the reality of God's kingdom. For example, in God's kingdom there would be no blind or lame, so Jesus made the blind see and the lame walk. Though most Jews did not accept Jesus as their long-awaited Messiah, some did.

In the years immediately after Jesus' resurrection, these followers of Jesus, all of whom were Jewish, had a problem. They proclaimed to all who would listen that Jesus truly was the long-expected Messiah, but it was also clear that evil and tragedy and suffering were still present in the world. It's as if the Messiah had come, but the Kingdom of God had not! To the average Jew, the answer was simple—Jesus wasn't really the Messiah, hence the world still awaited the coming of the Kingdom of God.

Already and not yet ... present and yet-to-come

But Jesus' disciples had seen, touched, and eaten with the risen Christ. They knew that God's anointed had indeed come. Jesus' resurrection was the proof of that. Thus, the problem was not with Jesus but with the Jewish perspective of the last days. In the writings of the New Testament, we see a new perspective emerging.

Yes, Jesus was the Messiah. Yes, God's kingdom had come—but not yet in all its fullness! The time of renewal had arrived with the Messiah's coming, but the consummation of this transformation would await his return. The Christians came to understand that they lived "between times" when God's kingdom had come *already,* but *not yet*. We don't mean partially now and fully later. We mean both now and later. Perplexing, yes.

Here's an example that may help. Not long ago, people spoke of a marriage being "consummated." Since marriage was seen as a becoming-one-flesh (Genesis 1:24), the couple wasn't really considered to be married until the time of their sexual union, the consummation. If such a sexual union never happened, then the marriage ceremony could be annulled, for the marriage had never really happened. So if the ceremony was at 3 p.m. but the honeymoon evening didn't get underway until midnight, and you asked the couple at 6 p.m. if they were married, they could honestly say they were married *already*, but *not yet*. At that moment, for those few hours, they were living in this odd "in-between time" when they were both married and not married. Not partially married—but truly married and not married at the same time.[39]

To reiterate, I can't overemphasize how important to our reading of the New Testament is understanding this "already/not yet" perspective. When Paul writes that Christians are the ones on whom the "ends of the ages have come" (1 Corinthians 10:11), he means exactly that!

This framework determined everything about the early Christians—how they lived, how they thought, what they

---

[39] Some years ago, a member of the St. Andrew congregation, Vicky Dearing, came up with this illustration in one of my classes and I've never found one that gets closer to the mark.

wrote, how they worshipped ... everything. The new order had begun. They were new creations (2 Corinthians 5:17). They were now the people of the Spirit. And, truly, so are we!

We are empowered by God's Spirit to live the life of the future, of God's kingdom, in the present age. We are to be, in Paul's phrase, "ambassadors for Christ," carrying God's message of reconciliation and hope to the world, in what we do and say every day. We are new creations not just for our own sakes but for the sake of the whole world.

Paul understood that in his journeys he was crisscrossing the Mediterranean founding colonies of a new human race, a people born from above, born of the Spirit (John 3). All Christian churches are just such colonies. It can be hard for us to think of ourselves this way, but that is the nature of transformation. It may take the butterfly awhile to comprehend its own rebirth. We may not always feel like new creations. We certainly don't always act like new creations. But we are ... already. *This is the real world.*

Part 2

The Essential Beliefs

What we believe and why it matters

The Apostles' Creed

I believe in God the Father Almighty,
maker of heaven and earth;
And in Jesus Christ his only Son our Lord:
who was conceived by the Holy Spirit,
born of the Virgin Mary,
suffered under Pontius Pilate,
was crucified, dead, and buried;
the third day he rose from the dead;
he ascended into heaven,
and sitteth at the right hand of God the Father Almighty;
from thence he shall come to judge the quick and the dead.
I believe in the Holy Spirit,
the holy catholic church,
the communion of saints,
the forgiveness of sins,
the resurrection of the body,
and the life everlasting. Amen.

I believe . . .

In the next seven chapters, we'll explore the Apostles' Creed, the affirmation of faith that Christians worldwide stand together and proclaim when we gather to worship. We'll begin by learning a bit about the creed's origin and purposes.

The origin of the Apostles' Creed

A creed is a statement of faith, a succinct and sometimes poetic presentation of the essentials of the Christian faith. A creed lays out the basic public proclamation that Christians present to the world.

The word "creed" is based on the Latin word *credo* which means "I believe" or "I trust" or "I have faith that ...."

From the earliest days of Christianity, we have used creeds of one sort or another to present and clarify the essentials. The creed expresses our "oneness" as the community of God's people. This is why we usually say it as a community, even though it begins "I believe...." Further, the creed's own "oneness" can be seen its Trinitarian outline: One God—Father, Son, and Holy Spirit.

When we come to the creeds it is always a good idea to remember one of Methodism founder John Wesley's favorite sayings: "In the essentials, unity; in all else, liberty; in everything, charity." A creed is simply meant to capture such essentials, about which all Christians ought to agree—really, *must* agree if the word "Christian" is to mean anything at all.

Christians have been standing and proclaiming the Apostles' Creed from the earliest centuries of Christianity. The Apostles' Creed grew out of the baptismal questions that people new to the faith were asked to affirm. Still today, those being baptized (or their sponsors) are asked to affirm certain statements of faith. Here are the baptismal questions from Rome dating back to at least AD 200:

- "Do you believe in God the Father Almighty?"
- "Do you believe in Jesus Christ, the Son of God, who was born of the Holy Spirit and the Virgin Mary, who was crucified under Pontius Pilate, and died, and rose on the third day living from the dead, and ascended into heaven, and sat down at the right hand of the Father, the one coming to judge the living and the dead?"
- "Do you believe in the Holy Spirit and the Holy Church and the resurrection of the flesh?"

We affirm every portion of every one of these questions whenever we stand to recite the Apostles' Creed.

The pros and cons of creeds

Not all Christian denominations embrace the historic creeds of the church, although nearly all have some statement of what they believe. Here are some of the pro's and con's when it comes to creeds:

Here are some of the pros:

> Creeds help us to clarify, proclaim, and protect the essential claims of our faith. Many creeds resulted from heretical threats to the faith. The creeds help us to recognize inadequate or incorrect descriptions of our faith.

> Creeds carry the tradition that we have received from the Christians who preceded us. Creeds remind us that there is one "cloud of saints."

> Creeds help provide us with a framework for interpreting Scripture and for teaching the basic Christian beliefs.

And some of the cons:

> Creeds can be used to exclude and enforce.
> No creed can substitute for our engagement with Scripture.
> No creed can be complete.
> No creed can be final.

The big picture

Take a look again at the Apostles' Creed. You'll quickly see that (1) it is Trinitarian, organized around the Father, Son, and Holy Spirit, and (2) it is narrative, beginning with creation and moving on to Jesus and then the church.

What's missing? A lot. First, you can't call the creed a summary of the biblical story, for where is any mention of Israel or the Law and the prophets? Second, nothing is stated outright about Jesus' divinity nor about the Spirit's divinity. This would come in the later creeds. For example, in the Nicene Creed of AD 325 (drafted to confront the claim that Jesus wasn't truly God), Jesus is "very God of very God, begotten not made, of one substance with the Father; through whom [Jesus] all things were made." Third, though the Apostles' creed affirms the forgiveness of sins, nothing is said specifically about how we are saved, and there is no mention of grace or faith.

When we say the creed we inevitably read a lot into it, but the creed is not meant to cover all the bases, just the essentials. It isn't the place for our "intramural" arguments about justification or sanctification or most of the important issues that we talk about in the church. The creed is meant to unite, not divide.

God the Father ...

I believe in God, the Father Almighty,
maker of heaven and earth. ...

Genesis 1:1-5 (NIV)

In the beginning God created the heavens and the earth.
[2] Now the earth was formless and empty, darkness was over
the surface of the deep, and the Spirit of God was hovering
over the waters.

[3] And God said, "Let there be light," and there was
light. [4] God saw that the light was good, and he separated
the light from the darkness. [5] God called the light "day," and
the darkness he called "night." And there was evening, and
there was morning—the first day.

Psalm 91:1-2 (NIV)

[1] Whoever dwells in the shelter of the Most High
   will rest in the shadow of the Almighty.
[2] I will say of the LORD, "He is my refuge and my fortress,
   my God, in whom I trust."

Matthew 7:7-11 (NIV)

[7] "Ask and it will be given to you; seek and you will find;
knock and the door will be opened to you. [8] For everyone

who asks receives; the one who seeks finds; and to the one who knocks, the door will be opened.

⁹ "Which of you, if your son asks for bread, will give him a stone? ¹⁰ Or if he asks for a fish, will give him a snake? ¹¹ If you, then, though you are evil, know how to give good gifts to your children, how much more will your Father in heaven give good gifts to those who ask him!

For nearly two millennia, Christians have proclaimed the essential truths about God and his work in this world. But what does this affirmation of faith really say to us about the nature of God? And what are its implications for us and our lives with one another and with God?

Though the Apostles' Creed is inherently Trinitarian, that doesn't mean the relational nature of God is well developed in it. The creed comes from a time when that theological work was still underway. Nonetheless, there are a few points that need to be made here.

First, because of Scripture's teachings on Jesus and the fact that the earliest Christians worshiped Jesus as they had worshiped God, the early church had to wrestle with some key questions:

- Is the Father, God? Is the Son, God? Is the Spirit, God?
- Is each person of the Trinity addressed by distinguishable divine names?

- Is each person assumed to have divine attributes?
- Does each person engage in actions that only God can accomplish?
- Is each person thought to be worthy of divine worship?

In each case, the church answered "yes." The mystery of the Trinity, one God of one "substance" yet three persons, is the most profound of all the mysteries we proclaim. Yet, it is absolutely essential to who we are and to the good news we proclaim to the world. And we are led to it every time we answer the question, "Who is Jesus?," as nearly all his disciples have answered it for 2,000 years.

Daniel Migliore lifts up for us three key Christian affirmations that arise from our belief in the Trinity:

- The eternal life of God is personal life in relationship. God *is* love (1 John 4:16b)—this makes sense only because of God's inherent relationality. God's identity is personal relationship.
- God exists in community. Yes, God has a social life. The three persons of God "indwell" each other. God then creates a people to live in relationship with him.
- The life of God is essentially self-giving love.

The Father

The portrait of God[40] as Father cuts across both Testaments. In the Old Testament, God is the Father of his people and the husband to his bride. But, in contrast to the New Testament, there are no prayers to the Father in the Hebrew Scriptures. God is simply referred to as *el* (the word for "god") or by God's name, YHWH (for which LORD is substituted in the English translations).[41]

There is often confusion around God and the Father. God is not synonymous with the Father. The Father is fully and completely God but is *not* all of God. The same is true of the Son and of the Holy Spirit. The Father is one of the three persons of the Trinity.

The Apostles' Creed probably exacerbates this problem in that it goes: "I believe in God the Father Almighty ... and in Jesus Christ ... in the Holy Spirit." Something like this would be more accurate: "I believe in God, and in the Father Almighty ... in Jesus Christ ... in the Holy Spirit."

---

[40] Allan Coppedge's book, *Portraits of God: A Biblical Theology of Holiness* (Downers Grove, Ill.: IVP Academic Press, 2001), is very helpful in seeing the larger picture of this "portrait" and others, such as "good shepherd" and "righteous judge." It is more a reference book than a read-straight-through book, but if you are interested in the full biblical witness to the metaphors used to talk about God, this book is a great resource.

[41] Though, in Jesus' day, "Father" was a common way to refer to the Lord God.

The New Testament has a much fuller expression of God as Father, emphasizing covenantal intimacy. Jesus even uses the familiar *abba* (sort of like "papa") to refer to the Father, and Paul urges all Christians to do the same. This parental portrait is one of the most intimate expressions of our relationship to God. As a teacher, I find the parent/child analogy to be one of the most important in seeking to understand our claims about God and how he works in this world.

God as Father encompasses two key tasks of fathers and, more broadly, parents. First, parents provide the child with standards, instruction, and discipline. Second, good parents shower their children with love, affection, encouragement, and support. Sadly, for too many Christians, difficult relationships with their human fathers make it difficult for them to come to God the Father and see someone who loves them and wants the best for them.

Almighty

"Almighty" translates the Latin *omnipotens* (omnipotent) and the Greek *pantokrator* (ruler of all things).[42] Interestingly, in the New Testament, "Almighty" is found only in Revelation. Obviously, however, just because the specific word *pantokrator* is rarely used, the affirmation that God is all-powerful and the ruler of all things is found from Genesis to Revelation.

Are we affirming that God can do anything? No! Could God lie? Could God act unjustly? To understand what we mean

---

[42] There were both Latin and Greek versions of the creed.

by saying that God is all-powerful, we must look to God's character, which is revealed in what God has done. And that is the story told by Scripture.

But we *are* affirming that God is in charge. This is God's cosmos. His purposes for his cosmos will be accomplished. But how God's sovereignty plays out is something that Christians have debated for two millennia and will continue to debate until Jesus returns. For example, how does God accomplish God's purposes but not trample all over our free will? In all our many discussions and even arguments, the affirmation that God is the "Almighty" reminds us that all of God's promises will be kept.

Maker of heaven and earth

Here, we affirm that God is the creator of all things. If it exists, God created it. The classic Christian doctrine is that God created everything *ex nihilo*, from nothing. There was no pre-existing raw material that God worked with. God simply created. And not just the material stuff of the cosmos, but the immaterial as well. Again, if it exists—at all, in any form—God created it. And God created it "good."[43]

True, the world is no longer *as* God created it. It has been terribly distorted and warped by sin and awaits its own redemption. Sickness, tragedy, death are all symptoms of this distortion. But still, God's purpose is to renew his creation, not destroy it.

---

[43] Thus, Christian theologians have been careful to state that evil is nothingness, i.e., not created, non-existent.

Why does this matter? It matters for more reasons than I could touch on here, but let's look at one. Embracing the goodness and the inherent value of God's creation helps us to understand and to accomplish the work God has given us. This world is not a place to be escaped from or even tolerated as we await our trip to heaven. Yes, the world is in much need of renewal and restoration. There is often little evidence of God's kingdom. But our charge is to do all we can to make God's kingdom evident to all. We can't build the kingdom—that is God's work—but we can build *for* the kingdom. Every kind touch, every mouth we feed and body we clothe, every act of selfless giving, every word of truth, every work of beauty we create, all compassion, all sacrifice—none of it will be lost, all of it will be incorporated into God's renewal of creation, a restoration of the physical *and* the spiritual.[44]

---

[44] N.T. Wright expressed this far better in a sermon entitled, "New Life—New World," from his book *Following Jesus* (Grand Rapids: Eerdmans, 1997). His sermon collections always make for worthwhile reading.

And in Jesus Christ . . .

"And in Jesus Christ his only Son our Lord,
who was conceived by the Holy Spirit,
born of the Virgin Mary . . .".

Hebrews 1:1-5 (NIV)

In the past God spoke to our ancestors through the prophets at many times and in various ways, ² but in these last days he has spoken to us by his Son, whom he appointed heir of all things, and through whom also he made the universe. ³ The Son is the radiance of God's glory and the exact representation of his being, sustaining all things by his powerful word. After he had provided purification for sins, he sat down at the right hand of the Majesty in heaven. ⁴ So he became as much superior to the angels as the name he has inherited is superior to theirs.

⁵ For to which of the angels did God ever say,

"You are my Son;
today I have become your Father"?
Or again,
"I will be his Father,
and he will be my Son"?

Matthew 1:18-25 (NRSV)

¹⁸Now the birth of Jesus the Messiah took place in this way. When his mother Mary had been engaged to Joseph,

but before they lived together, she was found to be with child from the Holy Spirit. [19]Her husband Joseph, being a righteous man and unwilling to expose her to public disgrace, planned to dismiss her quietly. [20]But just when he had resolved to do this, an angel of the Lord appeared to him in a dream and said, "Joseph, son of David, do not be afraid to take Mary as your wife, for the child conceived in her is from the Holy Spirit. [21]She will bear a son, and you are to name him Jesus, for he will save his people from their sins." [22]All this took place to fulfill what had been spoken by the Lord through the prophet:

[23]Look, the virgin shall conceive and bear a son,
and they shall name him Emmanuel,"

which means, "God is with us." [24]When Joseph awoke from sleep, he did as the angel of the Lord commanded him; he took her as his wife, [25]but had no marital relations with her until she had borne a son; and he named him Jesus.

We turn to the question, "Who is Jesus?"
Are we really ready to affirm him as the Messiah,
as the Lord, as God himself?

And so we return to Jesus. Yes, he is the one to whom all roads must, in the end, lead. In the third part of this book, we'll tackle the contentious question, "Is Jesus the Really the Only Way?" As we'll see, the answer is an inescapable "yes," so long as Jesus is who he claimed to be and who, for 2,000 years, almost all Christians have proclaimed him to be. Thus, we shouldn't be surprised that much of the Apostles' Creed is focused on Jesus. By the time we finish the section of the Apostles' Creed on Jesus, we'll have a much better idea of how to answer that question. Some of this will be obvious, some of it probably new to you.

There are six claims about Jesus in the opening section. When we recite the creed, we affirm that we trust all these are true— we believe them, we have faith in their truth.

- There was/is a man named Jesus.
- He is the Christ.
- He is God's only Son.
- He is Lord.
- His birth was conceived by the Holy Spirit.
- He was born to a woman named Mary who had never had sexual relations.

Let's take all six in order.

Jesus

Jesus' name focuses us on this particular man, given the name Yeshua ("Jesus" in English) at his birth. The name means "God saves" in Hebrew. Elsewhere in the Bible, the name is rendered as "Joshua." It was a common Jewish name in the first century. More will be said about this man, Jesus, but there will be nothing about where he is from or even about the bulk of his public ministry.

Christ

Though we often treat "Jesus Christ" as if they were the man's first and last names, "Christ" is actually a title. It translates the

Greek word, *christos*, which translates the Hebrew *masiah,* which means "the anointed one." Sometimes we take the Hebrew *masiah* more directly into English as "Messiah."

Though Israel and the law are not mentioned in the Apostles' Creed, this designation of Jesus as the Christ, the Messiah, brings in the Old Testament story, for the kings of Israel were referred to as "anointed ones," *masiahs.* By the time of Jesus there had not been a legitimate king of Israel from David's family for more than 500 years. The Jewish expectation was that God would raise up such a king and this man would usher in the long awaited kingdom of God, when all the world would see that the Jews had been right all along and would come to worship the one true God.

When reading the New Testament, it is critically important to understand that the Jews expected the Messiah to be a human and certainly not God himself. "Messiah" and "God" were two different persons, two different categories. Indeed, the fact that Christians claimed those two categories came together in the man named Jesus was a key reason why most Jews rejected Jesus and all the claims about him.

Naming Jesus as "Christ" at this point in the creed is not a claim to his divinity. It *does* claim that this Jesus is the one in whom the Old Testament story culminated and that his coming ushered in the kingdom of God.

His only Son

This is where it begins to get tricky. The Apostles' Creed merely claims that Jesus is God's only son. Naturally, we see in this a clear and definitive statement of Jesus' divinity. But the truth is that designating someone as a "son of God" wasn't necessarily such a claim. Read Genesis 6 to meet some rather far-out "sons of God." By the time of Jesus, it was increasingly believed that a Roman emperor was the son of a god—and some were the only son.

Now, I do think that those who originated the baptismal questions and answers from which this creed sprang intended to make a claim here about Jesus' divinity, but it wasn't long before the church leaders had to come back to this and write something much clearer. Here is the relevant passage from the Nicene Creed, written in AD 325:

> "We believe in one Lord, Jesus Christ, the only Son of God, eternally begotten of the Father, God from God, Light from Light, true God from true God, begotten, not made, of one Being with the Father. Through him all things were made."[45]

You can see my point. No one could possibly misread the claim in the Nicene Creed that, yes, Jesus is God and the phrase "his only Son" means just that.

---

[45] "Begotten" isn't a word we use much more anymore. Human children are begotten of human parents. Puppies are begotten of canine parents. We beget our own kind. Thus, to call Jesus God's only begotten Son is to make clear that he uniquely shares God's "DNA," to use an analogy.

Our Lord

A "lord" is a master, aka the boss. And that is exactly the claim for Jesus. In a sense, it speaks to his function. It, too, is not directly a claim to Jesus' divinity, to equating him with God. It is a term of exaltation, which refers to God raising Jesus in rank and power, lifting him up above all other persons. As will be made clear a bit later in the Apostles' Creed, Jesus is exalted to be Lord and Judge, to "sit at the right hand of God," which is a further expression of exaltation, as is the affirmation of Jesus' "ascension."

All this speaks less to Jesus' divinity than to his authority. The claim is that Jesus is in charge and the claim extends to all persons whether they acknowledge Jesus as Lord or not. The fact that Barack Obama is my president does not depend on my agreement or even knowledge. Likewise, Jesus is Lord of every person on the planet, whether they've heard of him or not.

We need to hear the political challenge in claiming that Jesus is Lord. In the Roman Empire, which stretched from the British Isles to the Tigris and Euphrates rivers, everyone was under the rule and authority of Julius Caesar. He called the shots, determining even who lived and who died. Caesar was Lord. That's just how it was. There can be only one Lord above all lords and that was Caesar. He was the king of kings.

But the Christians claimed that Jesus was Lord, that he was the one who commanded their ultimate allegiance. Not Caesar, Jesus. And so do we. Every time we stand to say the creed, we affirm that Jesus is not only our Lord, our master, we claim that he is the Lord of everyone. And as Lord, Jesus shares in the honor that is God's and is to be obeyed as God is to be obeyed. So much in one little word!

Conceived by the Holy Spirit, born of the Virgin Mary

I combined these two phrases for a simple reason: they are best seen as two sides of a single coin, and that coin is Jesus. These two statements are claims that Jesus is divine ("conceived by the Holy Spirit") and human ("born of the Virgin Mary"). Truly God and truly human.

These claims proved to be some of the most contentious among Christians. Some claimed that Jesus was the person closest to God, even the most Godlike, but not really and truly God. Others claimed that he only appeared to be human, but wasn't really, truly human like you and me.

These controversies raged across the Christian communities in the early centuries and gave rise to the great creeds, for such questions lie at the heart of our beliefs about the Trinitarian nature of God. If Jesus is truly God, then aren't there two gods, but then again, aren't we monotheistic, and so on. You can imagine the late night discussions and mental headaches that arose from such questions.

As noted before, the Apostles' Creed is so brief that early church leaders had to write more. The later and fuller Nicene Creed sets forth Jesus' full and undiminished divinity. Here is how:

For us and for our salvation he came down from heaven; by the power of the Holy Spirit he became incarnate from the Virgin Mary, and became truly human.[46]

Fully God and fully human?

Try to get your brain around that for a minute. It isn't surprising that the Christian community has always had to work through well-meaning but misguided attempts to explain how Jesus could be really, truly God and really, truly human at the same time. How could one person have two natures, divine and human?

As I've mentioned briefly, one proposed solution was to deny that Jesus was truly God. Another was to deny that Jesus was truly human. Great councils of the church met to explain why these are serious errors that undercut the gospel.

Here are a few more ways we can get this wrong:

For some, the mystery is solved by seeing Jesus as having only one, unique nature, a hybrid of sorts—the unique "God-man." Of course, then he wouldn't be truly God or truly human. It would be as if Jesus was a third "species." He is not; he is fully God *and* fully human.

---

[46] You can see that the vocabulary of theologians begins to make its appearance; in this case, "incarnate," which means "in the flesh." Jesus is God incarnate, God in the flesh.

Another way is to suggest that Jesus had a truly human body, but lacked a human rational mind or soul, instead being filled with the divine Logos/Word. Jesus then becomes "God in a bod," again losing his true humanity. There is much more to being human than these bags of blood and bones that hold us up.

Or perhaps Jesus is a perfect "moral union," much like persons in a perfect marriage. One nature doing the "God stuff" and one nature doing the "human stuff." Of course, he is then only half God and half human. For good reason, the church councils insisted that Jesus' two natures are inseparable—not a right and left or top and bottom.

Or still another choice: "Jesus' humanity was like a drop of wine in an ocean of his divinity." But then what remains of Jesus' humanity? How can we speak of a "drop of humanity" in the Garden of Gethsemane? Jesus was fully and completely human. He was the most human human.[47]

It would be a mistake to see all this as so much pointless speculation. Christians have always known that answering the question, "Who is Jesus?" lies at the very heart of the gospel. Almost all of the great heresies that have arisen in the last two millennia are centered on this question. Christianity's tensions with other religions all center on this question.

---

[47] It is an odd thing that when we mess up badly, we often say something like, "I'm just being human." The truth is that when we are at our worst we are not being more human, we are being less human.

Christians of all stripes have wrestled with Scripture, trying to make sense of what is revealed there about Jesus. Yes, "In the beginning was the Word and the Word was with God and the Word was God" (John 1:1). And yes, Jesus was born to a young woman from a small village in Galilee. The creed writers didn't invent anything, they simply brought together the core teachings and practices of the early church. Their language expressed, in increasingly precise terms, those teachings and practices.

The great Christian confessions uphold two inseparable natures, divine and human, in one person, Jesus—sort of two "whats" and one "who."[48] How can this be? Trying too hard to answer that question has led inevitably to distortions of Jesus and of the gospel.

The great cloud of witnesses to the good news urges us to stay true to the full revelation of Scripture and avoid some understandable mistakes: don't deny the full divinity and the full humanity of Jesus; don't divide him into two persons; don't make him into some hybrid "God-man." Instead, embrace and proclaim the Jesus-Who-Is, not a Jesus of our own making, even if we can't penetrate all the mysteries of God.

---

[48] Using "what/nature" and "who/person," Jesus is two "whats" (two natures, human and divine) and one "who" (Jesus). We can speak of the Trinity as one "what" (a single divine nature) and three "whos" (Father, Son, and Holy Spirit).

Suffered under Pontius Pilate

suffered under Pontius Pilate,
was crucified, dead, and buried;
[he descended into hell.]"

from Mark 15 (NRSV)

As soon as it was morning, the chief priests held a consultation with the elders and scribes and the whole council. They bound Jesus, led him away, and handed him over to Pilate. ...

... ¹⁵So Pilate, wishing to satisfy the crowd, released Barabbas for them; and after flogging Jesus, he handed him over to be crucified.

¹⁶Then the soldiers led him into the courtyard of the palace (that is, the governor's headquarters); and they called together the whole cohort. ¹⁷And they clothed him in a purple cloak; and after twisting some thorns into a crown, they put it on him. ¹⁸And they began saluting him, "Hail, King of the Jews!" ¹⁹They struck his head with a reed, spat upon him, and knelt down in homage to him. ²⁰After mocking him, they stripped him of the purple cloak and put his own clothes on him. Then they led him out to crucify him.

... ²⁴And they crucified him, and divided his clothes among them, casting lots to decide what each should take. ... ³⁴At three o'clock Jesus cried out with a loud voice, "Eloi, Eloi, lema sabachthani?" which means, "My God, my God, why have you forsaken me?"... ³⁷Then Jesus gave a loud cry and breathed his last. ...

... ⁴³Joseph of Arimathea, a respected member of the council, who was also himself waiting expectantly for the kingdom of God, went boldly to Pilate and asked for the body of Jesus. ... ⁴⁵When he [Pilate] learned from the centurion that he was dead, he granted the body to Joseph. ⁴⁶Then Joseph bought a linen cloth, and taking down the body, wrapped it in the linen cloth, and laid it in a tomb that had been hewn out of the rock. He then rolled a stone against the door of the tomb.

If you were going to tell someone about Jesus' life from the day after his birth until the day he died, and you had to do it in nine words, what would they be?

Here's the thing about Christianity. Ours is not a religion grounded upon ideas or philosophies, nor upon traditions or practices. Rather, Christianity is grounded upon the truthfulness of certain historical claims. We don't begin by developing a workable theology of the Trinity nor even a so-called "proof" of God's existence. We begin by pointing at history—actual places, actual times, actual people—saying, "Look at what God has done!" Look: this man, Jesus, from Galilee has been resurrected, brought through death to new life. Look: see, hear, touch, listen, smell.

Here's an excellent and very early example. When some Christians in Corinth, Greece, question Paul about whether Jesus was actually resurrected, Paul doesn't engage in an intellectually stimulating conversation about how such a thing could be. Instead, he simply starts listing off witnesses to the truth of the historical event, culminating in a challenge to go and talk to one of the 500 or so witnesses about *what actually happened*. Paul understands quite well that if it didn't happen, if Jesus wasn't truly resurrected to new life, then all—yes, all—Christianity is a lie and Christians are to be pitied more than anyone for putting their trust in such a lie.

Indeed, Paul puts his claims quite succinctly: "For I handed on to you as of first importance what I in turn had received: that Christ died for our sins in accordance with the scriptures, and that he was buried, and that he was raised on the third day in accordance with the scriptures ...." (1 Corinthians 15:3-5). Bear in mind that Paul wrote this letter only about twenty-five years after Jesus' death and resurrection, yet already Paul is passing on the basic claims in a creedal form.

You see, Christianity—all that we proclaim in the good news and more, *all of it*—stands or falls on the actual historical truthfulness of the claim that God raised Jesus to new life. The claim isn't really all that complicated once you learn what "resurrection" meant in the Greco-Roman world. It may or not have happened, but the claim is straightforward. As is this entire section of the creed.

Beginning with the phrase "born to the Virgin Mary," we learn that this man Jesus with the mother named Mary suffered at the hands of Pontius Pilate (whom we know was the Roman

Prefect of Judea from AD 26 to AD 36, during the reign of Tiberius, Emperor of Rome). We also learn that Pilate handed Jesus over to be crucified (a particularly shameful and horrible way to execute those seen as opposing Roman rule). Jesus died, of course, for the Roman death squads were efficient if nothing else. And Jesus was then buried, in accordance with the burial practices of first-century Jews. All this we learn from the pages of the gospel accounts.

Suffered?

All four gospels recount in excruciating detail the suffering that Jesus endured in the hours before his death. But why include it in the creed? It is true, but could there be important theological claims here as well as historical claims?

Certainly, it affirms the price that Jesus paid for our salvation. And, like so much in this section of the creed, it affirms his genuine humanity. We humans know far too much about suffering.

But what about Jesus' divinity? Could we possibly conclude that God suffered that day?

Many Christians over the last two millenia would answer resoundingly "No!" Would not a suffering God be a diminished God, diminished in God's good perfection? Isn't God above our suffering and distress? The Council of Chalcedon in AD 451 condemned those who believed that God could suffer. Augustine and John Calvin also denied the possibility of

God's suffering. There is a big theological word for this: the *impassibility*[49] of God, i.e., God cannot suffer.

But this is not really the biblical view. Instead, it is drawn more from the Greek philosophers, for whom the "One" was not at all personal. Rather, the "Prime Mover" was perfection. Look at this list of adjectives and you'll have no trouble knowing which is drawn from Scripture and which from Plato.

• Loving	• Omniscient
• Faithful	• Omnipotent
• Compassionate	• Omnipresent
• Relentless	• Transcendent
• Just	• Immutable
• Merciful	• Impassible

Those who defend the impassibility of God will sometimes talk about Jesus' suffering in his human nature, but not his divine nature. However, such a notion diminishes the inseparability of Jesus' two natures—he is not two separate halves joined or commingled in one body. Jesus is one person with two inseparable natures.

If Jesus suffered—as he most assuredly did—Jesus suffered in his human and his divine natures. In addition, what sort of Father doesn't suffer as his only Son is nailed to a cross? Not a

---

[49] The term "impassibility" is drawn from the Latin *passio*, which was used for the suffering of Christ in the Vulgate, the Latin version of the Bible translated in about AD 400. The Greek word for suffering is *paschō*.

Father I wish to know or emulate and certainly not the Father I meet in Scripture.

Dennis Ngien writes:

> Our Christian foreparents were right to speak of God as impassible if that means God is not emotionally unstable and cannot be manipulated by humans. But they were wrong to conclude from this that God has no passion. They were wrong to think a suffering God is an imperfect being who necessarily seeks his perfection and tries to overcome his deficiency though actions. C. S. Lewis makes a helpful distinction between "gift love" (agape) and "need love" (eros). God does not act out of need love—a love dominated by self-seeking desires. Rather, God acts out of gift love—a free, self-giving love—sharing his boundless goodness without thought of return. God's goodness means that he loves us with a completely unconditional love, involving himself with us even in our pain.[50]

Our proclamation to the world of the God-Who-Suffers is unique among the world's religions and seems downright foolish to many. But as Paul wrote to the Corinthians: "The message about the cross is foolishness to those who are perishing, but to us who are being saved it is the power of God" (1 Cor. 1:18).

---

[50] From Ngien's excellent article, "The God Who Suffers," in *Christianity Today*, February 3, 1997.

What an odd, wonderful, strange, compassionate, surprising, loving God it is who loves us.

Crucified?

The basics are straightforward. Crucifixion was simply the most horrible way the Romans had available to publicly torture those who opposed Rome. The process of dying was painful and often went on for several days. The mounting of the victim on the cross ensured that death came by slow suffocation if not by shock, for as the dying person grew increasingly unable to lift themselves they could no longer expand their lungs and breathe.

The Romans did not invent crucifixion but they did perfect it and used it more widely than any empire before them. Crucifixion was not the death typically meted out to common criminals; it was generally reserved for those who stood up to the power of Rome. Thus, for example, when Jesus was a boy, several thousand Galilean Jews were crucified along the roadways to put down a rebellion against Roman authority. The sign over Jesus' head that read "King of the Jews" marked him as someone who was crucified as a challenger to the power of Caesar.

But why is it in the creed? Why not simply state that Jesus was executed? Why specify the form of execution? First, it grounds the creed in the actual history, for the specific form of execution *was* crucifixion. Second, it inevitably acknowledges that, by virtues of his claims to lordship, Jesus did oppose Caesar and his empire.

Third, and I think the hardest for us to comprehend, is that this affirmation lifts Jesus up as having suffered the most humiliating and shameful possible death. Crucifixion was so horrific that it couldn't even be mentioned in polite company. For a culture built upon the acquisition of honor and the avoidance of shame, this aspect of crucifixion might well have been the most awful in the eyes of many.

Paul captures this humiliation well when, speaking of Jesus, he wrote, "he humbled himself and became obedient to the point of death—even death on a cross" (Philippians 2:8).

Jesus is flogged by Pilate's soldiers, mocked and spat upon. They put a crown of thorns on his head. But the one word affirmation "crucified" tells us all we could stand to know about the price Jesus paid for his faithfulness to God, to his vocation, to you, and to me.

Dead, and buried?

The process of burying practiced by Jews in Jesus' day was quite different from our own. The dead were not "buried" in graves. Instead the bodies were laid out in tombs until such time that the dried out bones could be collected and put in a bone box for storage.

But the process isn't really the point here. Why do we bother saying that Jesus was both dead and buried? Isn't that a bit redundant?

Yes, it is redundant and that is exactly the point. We are affirming that Jesus' crucifixion resulted in his death, that Jesus was dead, dead, and dead. No swooning or fainting from which Jesus later recovered. Not merely near death or all-but-dead. Jesus was dead—just as all humans die. No heart beat. No brain waves. Dead. ... guess I've been clear. The Roman death squad accomplished its task. Indeed, to suggest that they failed in their assigned task is mere fancy. The soldiers knew how to kill and were well-acquainted with death.

So why is this affirmation so important? Because the creed is about to make an astonishing claim, that this dead man, Jesus, was resurrected by God!

There is one more point to be made about Jesus' death that hearkens back to last chapter. Jesus died, just as all of us die. He was fully and completely human. The laws of physics and biology applied to him just as to us. But, you may ask, isn't he also fully and completely God? And if so, are we saying that God died?

In a way, yes. It is inescapable that one person of the Trinity, Jesus, dies on that cross. But did the Father die? No. The Spirit? No. So ... what does all this mean? ... Beats me. I just know that Jesus died. Not just part of him, but all of him. In the end, it is a fool's errand to try to figure out all the mysteries of God.

Descended into hell?

This final phrase isn't typically said in many denominations and churches, though it is often footnoted in hymnals and such. However, some still include the phrase and I'm often asked why we in the United Methodist Church tend to leave it out. I think that some folks wonder if it is because we afraid to mention "hell."

No, that isn't the reason at all. We don't say it because the language is misleading and Christians don't even agree on how the phrase ought to be understood. These problems have been discussed and debated nearly since the creed's creation. But the problem has gotten worse in recent centuries.

The basic problem is this: As originally created, the Apostles' Creed affirms that "Jesus descended into *Hades*," which is the Greek name for the place of the dead in the ancient cosmology. J. I. Packer, noted conservative Evangelical scholar, writes:

> The English is misleading, for "hell" has changed its sense since the English form of the Creed was fixed. Originally, "hell" meant the place of the departed as such, corresponding to the Greek *Hades* and the Hebrew *Sheol*. That is what it means here, where the Creed echoes Peter's statement that Psalm 16:10, "for you do not give me up to Sheol," was a prophecy fulfilled when Jesus rose (see Acts 2:27-31). But since the seventeenth century "hell" has been used to signify only the state of final retribution for the godless, for which the New Testament name is *Gehenna*.[51]

---

[51] Packer, J. I., *Growing in Christ* (Wheaton, Ill.: Crossway Books, 1996), 56.

That's the problem. We hear "hell," and we think of a place of final punishment. But all the creed meant was the place of the dead. And what did Jesus do there? This has been a source of much debate over centuries. Bruce Lockerbie sums it up this way:

> To some, the descent into hell represents the physical agony of death upon the Cross. It was hellish in its pain. To others, the word hell means Hades or Sheol, the collective abode of the dead, divided into Paradise or Abraham's Bosom—the state of God-fearing souls—and Gehenna, the state of ungodly souls. Thus the descent into hell may suggest that the Son of God carried the sins of the world to hell; or the Son of God carried good news of deliverance to the godly dead such as Lazarus the beggar and the repentant thief.

> Still others believe that the descent into hell accounts for the problem of God's justice by providing an opportunity for all mankind—in eternity as well as in time—to hear the message of redemption from the Word Himself. But whatever interpretation one accepts, the scriptural passages upon which this teaching is based must be studied closely. Some of the standard texts are Job 38:17, Psalm 68:18-22; Matthew 12:38-41; Acts 2:22-32; Romans 10:7; Ephesians 4:7-10, 1 Peter 3:18-20, and 1 Peter 4:6.[52]

---

[52] From D. Bruce Lockerbie's *The Apostle's Creed: Do You Really Believe It* (Wheaton, Ill.: Victor Books, 1977), 53-54.

In my view, it makes sense to leave this phrase out of the creed. Creeds ought to be succinct, conveying only those affirmations about which nearly Christians can agree on the meaning.

A Bit More

Burial practices in Jesus' day

A close reading of the various gospel accounts of Jesus' death, burial, and resurrection can often be confusing to us because we don't know the basics of first-century Jewish burial practices. For example, did you ever wonder exactly what they were doing when they "buried" Jesus on Friday? Is there a six-foot-deep grave waiting for Jesus' body? Why are the women there on Sunday? Why is there a stone that can be rolled away?

Here's the big surprise: the Jews of Jesus' day practiced a two-stage burial. When a person died, family members would wrap the body in cloth and place it on a ledge in a cave or a manmade, family tomb. Perhaps a year or so later, when the body had decomposed, the family would return to the tomb and place the loved one's bones in a box. The "bone box," called an ossuary, would then be labeled and stored in a crypt along with the bone boxes of other family members.

As for Jesus, he was crucified and died on Friday afternoon. Because Jews could not touch a dead body on the Sabbath, which began at sundown on Friday, Mary and the others had to move quickly. Jesus' body was taken down from the cross, quickly wrapped in some linen, and then carried to an unused tomb that belonged to Joseph of Arimathea. Like most such tombs, a round stone was used to block to the entrance. The stone would keep animals out but still enable the family to come and go as they tended to the bodies and bones.

There, Jesus' wrapped body was laid on a stone slab. The women planned to return at dawn on Sunday, after resting on the Sabbath, to finish preparing Jesus' body for the year or more it would lie in the tomb. Why women? Because dead bodies were seen as "unclean" by the Jews, and handling them was left to the women, who were second-class citizens in the patriarchal cultures of the ancient world.

The third day he rose . . .

The third day he rose from the dead;
he ascended into heaven,
and sitteth at the right hand of God the Father Almighty;
from thence he shall come to judge the quick and the dead."

Acts 2:32-36 (NIV)

[32] God has raised this Jesus to life, and we are all witnesses of it. [33] Exalted to the right hand of God, he has received from the Father the promised Holy Spirit and has poured out what you now see and hear. [34] For David did not ascend to heaven, and yet he said,

"'The Lord said to my Lord:
"Sit at my right hand
[35] until I make your enemies
a footstool for your feet." '

[36] "Therefore let all Israel be assured of this: God has made this Jesus, whom you crucified, both Lord and Messiah."

2 Corinthians 5:6-10 (NIV)

[6] Therefore we are always confident and know that as long as we are at home in the body we are away from the Lord. [7] For we live by faith, not by sight. [8] We are confident, I say, and would prefer to be away from the body and at home with the Lord. [9] So we make it our goal to please him, whether

we are at home in the body or away from it. ¹⁰ For we must all appear before the judgment seat of Christ, so that each of us may receive what is due us for the things done while in the body, whether good or bad.

Why do we worship Jesus of Nazareth?
These affirmations make the answer crystal clear.

Now, we come to the final affirmations about Jesus in the Apostles' Creed. There are four key claims made:

- Jesus was resurrected on the third day after his death.
- Jesus returned to heaven.
- Jesus was exalted by God.
- Jesus is the judge before whom all will stand.

"On the third day ..."

The first claim is both astounding and straightforward. We affirm that on the third day[53] after his death on the cross, Jesus was bodily resurrected. The wording of the creed could be clearer, in that it uses the passive voice, leaving the reader unclear as to exactly who is accomplishing the resurrection. Did Jesus raise himself? The answer is no. Jesus was dead

---

[53] The claim isn't that 72 hours elapsed, but simply that Jesus died on a Friday and was resurrected on a Sunday—three days: Friday, Saturday, and Sunday.

and buried, as the creed affirms. Dead people can't resurrect themselves. It is God who raised Jesus.[54]

Most Jews of Jesus' day believed that God would bodily resurrect all the dead when the last days arrived and God put all things to rights. However, most Jews could not accept the claim that God had resurrected this one man only, this Galilean Jew who had died an humiliating death by crucifixion.

The Greeks, too, spoke of resurrection, *anastasis,* but they believed it could never happen. They could conceive of resurrection, but they knew that the dead stay dead. For the Greeks and Jews alike, resurrection meant newly embodied life after death. It would be like Achilles returning from Hades or Joshua from Sheol.[55]

There is one point here about which we need to be *absolutely clear,* for I hear Christians getting this wrong all the time.

We are *not* talking about resuscitation, being brought back from the dead to return to one's life (as on a modern-day operating

---

[54] Yes, Jesus is God, but that isn't the same as saying Jesus resurrected himself. If we try to express this in Trinitarian terms, we might be tempted to say that the resurrection of Jesus was the work of the Father or the Spirit. But Scripture isn't always explicit or consistent in such things. Thus, Christians have always spoken simply of God acting and speaking, for God is both truly three (persons) and one (divine being). Diversity and unity. Each of the three persons of the Trinity are fully and completely God, but none are all of God. There is one God who is not merely the sum of the three persons. Yes, it is okay if you don't quite see how this can be. No one can.

[55] These are the abodes of the dead in these ancient cosmologies.

table) and still having to face death. This was Lazarus: Jesus brought him back to life, but Lazarus returned to his home, aged, and died. The same is true of all the people in the Bible who are brought *back* to life.

In contrast, we claim that Jesus was resurrected by God, not merely resuscitated. He passed *through* death to a life after death (Friday evening to early Sunday morning) and then to newly embodied life on Sunday.[56] Jesus will not face death again. Jesus is the *only* person in the Bible that was resurrected.

From the perspective of Jesus' disciples by the act of resurrection God had done for Jesus what God will one day do for everyone. That's why Paul uses an agricultural metaphor to describe Jesus as the "first fruits of those who have died" (1 Cor. 15:20), the first person, but not the only person, to be resurrected.

It is understandable that Christians tend to see the resurrection as the place of God's victory, the climax of the biblical story. We are Easter people, after all. It is why the early Christians began to worship on Sunday, rather than on the Jewish Sabbath of Saturday. However, this is not the perspective of the New Testament writers.

In the New Testament, Jesus' resurrection is neither the place of God's victory over sin and death nor the climax of the story. Rather, the victory is won by Jesus' faithfulness all the way to

---

[56] N.T. Wright uses such a delightful turn of phrase here. He speaks of Jesus' and, hence, our own "life after life-after-death."

his death on the cross. Jesus' death is the atoning sacrifice that makes us "at-one" with God.

Using a variety of images, the New Testament writers concentrate on what Jesus' suffering and death has accomplished, i.e, we are reconciled to God, justified, put into a right relationship with God, declared innocent in a law court, returned from exile, forgiven our sins, pardoned, redeemed, etc. However, the New Testament does not give us a single theory of *how* this was accomplished.

The resurrection then is the *proof* that these claims are so. The resurrection demonstrates that Jesus was who he claimed to be, not merely another failed would-be messiah who met a bad end. The resurrection is the vindication of Jesus and, thus, the claim upon which the truth claims of Christianity stand or fall.

Finally, the resurrection demonstrates that we worship a promise-keeping God who has created, is creating, and will create again. It is as if the fulfillment of all God's promises about the restoration of humanity and the cosmos come forward to that Sunday morning when Jesus walked out of an empty tomb.

"Ascended into heaven"

This, too, may seem a very simple, straightforward statement and, in a way, it is. But I think we tend to miss its meaning. In the ancient cosmology, the gods are "up there," and the higher humans could get above the ground, the closer they were to the gods.[57] Thus, when Jesus leaves the disciples to return to God's place, he ascends skyward (see Acts 1). If Jesus was going to return to the Father, then the disciples would expect him to head off into the clouds, just as it is recounted in the book of Acts.

Of course, we know more now about the structure of the cosmos God has created. If we head skyward, we end up in outer space and, eventually, pass through other galaxies.[58]

Thus, this phrase in the creeds isn't a claim about Jesus heading off to a particular spot in space-time. Instead, it is a claim about Jesus' vindication (being proved right) and exaltation (being elevated in rank and power). The ascension language of the New Testament is exaltation language. Thus, the simple statement about Jesus' ascending is of a single piece with the next statement.

---

[57] As in the story of the Tower of Babel (Genesis 11), the pyramids, and the Babylonian ziggurats.

[58] Let's set aside the curvature of space-time; it will just make our heads hurt! This is not a physics lesson. I also wonder what folks a few hundred years from now will be saying about our understanding of the cosmos. I have this feeling that we don't know as much as we think we know.

"Sitteth at the right hand of God the Father Almighty"

Who's your boss? Your neighbors' boss? How about the folks an ocean away? Who is ultimately in charge of this planet we call earth? It is Jesus, regardless of whether everyone has heard of him or acknowledges that he is in charge. You might say to yourself, "Okay, but it sure seems like the inmates are running the asylum!" And at times, even most of the time, it sure does. How much must Jesus value our freedom, how essential it must be to the cosmos that God created. We are given a lot of freedom, but it is still Jesus who is Lord, who sits at the right hand of God in power and might and glory.

With this phrase about God's right hand, the exaltation of Jesus is further amplified and wraps back upon the earlier affirmation that Jesus is Lord. The phrase itself is simply a very Old Testament way of speaking of God's throne room, where one is given lordship and dominion by God, as in Psalm 110:1, "The Lord says to my lord, 'Sit at my right hand until I make your enemies your footstool.'" Jesus quotes this verse to Caiaphas at his trial, along with Daniel 7:13-14, another throne room image. It is a way of affirming that Jesus has taken his place as King of Kings and Lord of Lords.

Thus, when we come to these phrases of the Creed, we need to hear them as Jesus' glorification (lifting up for all to see that he is Messiah, Lord, and, indeed, God himself):

> ➢ crucifixion => resurrection => ascension=> seated at God's right hand

It is like a glorification arc and compels us to acknowledge that Jesus is to be worshipped as God is worshipped, and obeyed as God is obeyed.[59]

Judging the quick and dead

No, this is not about being speedy. "Quick" is simply an archaic wording[60] referring to being alive. Thus, we are affirming that Jesus will be the judge of everyone who has ever lived or is living when the day of judgment comes.

I don't know about you, but the whole idea of being judged leaves me pretty cold. Who wants to be judged? It is a word we associate with some very unfortunate portraits of God that too many people embrace. Thomas Matthews, an American journalist, writes:

> "I still think of God—no, not think, but apprehend, as I was trained as a child to envision him—as a watchful, vengeful, enormous, omniscient policeman, instantly aware of the

---

[59] It is important to reiterate that the Apostles' Creed comes from the early centuries of Christianity, when believers were still working out even the basics of a Trinitarian understanding of God.

[60] Many churches use this traditional, even archaic wording, because it links us to the billions of Christians who have come before us, most of whom have stood and said this creed and others just as we do.

slightest tinge of irreverence in my innermost thought, always ready to pounce if I curse, if I mention him in anger, fun, or mere habit … but how can that kind of fear of that kind of God be the beginning of wisdom?"[61]

Many Christians find that they hold a view of God, even of God the Father, that lines up pretty well with that of Thomas Matthews. At a minimum, they think that is what the Old Testament teaches about God and they contrast it with Jesus, almost pitting Jesus against the "God of the Old Testament."

Yet, if Jesus is who we claim him to be, fully and completely God, then how could Jesus be anything other than the full revelation of God? The problem lies in our poor and truncated reading of the Old Testament.

The need for there to be a final judge, who confronts and punishes those who do evil, beats strong in the human heart. We know that those who do the most terrible things do not always stand to account. We want them to be judged. If not in this life, then in the next.

When it comes to ourselves, of course, we recoil at the notion of standing to account for the lives we've lived. Yet the Bible is clear about this: we shall stand before the judge.

---

[61] From Terence Fretheim's *The Suffering of God: An Old Testament Perspective* (Minneapolis: Fortress Press, 1984).

But look who it is! We stand before the bar and discover that the judge is Jesus. What a relief. Then we look to our side and see that our advocate, our lawyer, is Jesus (1 John 2:1). Double relief. And then we realize that someone is tugging at our sleeve so we will step aside and let him stand in our place[62] (2 Cor. 5:21). Who? Jesus! Relief beyond measure.

This simple phrase from the creed is a song of hope and joy. Yes, there will be judgment, as there must and should be, but the judge is Jesus. Could we imagine Jesus *not* judging with love and justice and mercy? When we profess to be Christians we are saying that we've placed our full faith and trust in Jesus Christ. Not only as our savior and redeemer, but as our judge and, indeed, the judge of all—the living and the dead. Amen to that!

---

[62] This is the substitutionary theory of the atonement, one of a variety of such images in Scripture about how we are made right with God. Many Protestants make the mistake of seeing this as pretty much the only image of atonement, rather than as one amongst several.

The Holy Spirit, the holy catholic Church

*I believe in the Holy Spirit,
the holy catholic church, . . ".*

Isaiah 63:9-14 (NIV)

[9] In all their distress he too was distressed,
>and the angel of his <u>presence</u> saved them.

In his love and mercy he redeemed them;
>he lifted them up and carried them
>all the days of old.

[10] Yet they rebelled
>and grieved his <u>Holy Spirit</u>.

So he turned and became their enemy
>and he himself fought against them.

[11] Then his people recalled the days of old,
>the days of Moses and his people—
>where is he who brought them through the sea,
>with the shepherd of his flock?

Where is he who set
>his <u>Holy Spirit</u> among them,

[12] who sent his glorious arm of power
>to be at Moses' right hand,
>who divided the waters before them,
>to gain for himself everlasting renown,

[13] who led them through the depths?

Like a horse in open country,
>they did not stumble;

¹⁴ like cattle that go down to the plain,
>   they were given rest by the <u>Spirit of the LORD</u>.
> This is how you guided your people
>   to make for yourself a glorious name.

John 16:7-14 (NRSV)

⁷ Nevertheless I tell you the truth: it is to your advantage that I go away, for if I do not go away, the Advocate will not come to you; but if I go, I will send **him** to you. ⁸ And when **he** comes, **he** will prove the world wrong about sin and righteousness and judgment: ⁹ about sin, because they do not believe in me; ¹⁰ about righteousness, because I am going to the Father and you will see me no longer; ¹¹ about judgment, because the ruler of this world has been condemned.

¹² "I still have many things to say to you, but you cannot bear them now. ¹³ When the Spirit of truth comes, **he** will guide you into all the truth; for **he** will not speak on **his** own, but will speak whatever **he** hears, and **he** will declare to you the things that are to come. ¹⁴ **He** will glorify me, because **he** will take what is mine and declare it to you.

Now we come to the Holy Spirit, the third person of the Trinity, and certainly the least understood. Yet, it is the Spirit who is God. Present with us every day and it is the Spirit who has formed us into a holy and universal fellowship of believers.

The Apostles' Creed is about as simple and straightforward a statement of essential Christian beliefs as there is. Nonetheless, there are many Christians who don't really understand all of what they are affirming, why they are doing so, and what difference it makes. When we come to the Holy Spirit, there is a lot of misunderstanding and confusion that needs to be swept away. So here are a few Holy Spirit FAQs:

Exactly what is the Holy Spirit?

Yikes! First, the Holy Spirit is not a "what," but a "who." You, too, are not a "what" but a "who," a person. The Holy Spirit is a person. Look, for example, at the above passage from John 16. I've underlined all the personal pronouns that refer to the Holy Spirit, aka the Advocate.[63] The Spirit is no less a person than you and I.

In the Bible, the Spirit *searches, knows, teaches, dwells, accomplishes, gives life, cries out, bears witness, has desires, is grieved, helps, intercedes, works all things together, strengthens,* and is *lied to.* These are not verbs we apply to chairs or to electricity. The Holy Spirit is not akin to the Force of *Star Wars;* the Spirit is a person, a Holy Who! Don't be misled by the fact that the Bible uses images like doves, wind, or fire in reference to the Spirit. Such images illustrate something about the Spirit to us, but that is all. Scripture also refers to God as a "rock" and Jesus as a "door."

---

[63] Don't get too caught up in the fact that these are all masculine pronouns. In English, we only have "he" and "she" to choose from when it comes to singular personal pronouns. Using "it" is a far worse choice, for though it avoids the gender issues, it makes the Spirit seem impersonal.

But is the Spirit more like an angel or more like God?

The Holy Spirit is not an angel. Angels are created beings that are neither human nor divine. In Scripture, God uses angels as his messengers. Like you and me, angels are persons, though not divine.

And the Spirit is not merely "like God," the Holy Spirit *is* God, fully and completely, though not all of God. The Spirit is God in exactly the same manner as Jesus is God and the Father is God. These persons, the three "who's" of the Trinity, comprise the one God, who is not divisible, for God is one.[64]

Does the Holy Spirit have a name?

The name most commonly used by the New Testament writers is "the Holy Spirit." However, the Holy Spirit is also called "the Spirit," "the Spirit of God," "the Spirit of the Lord," "the Spirit of Christ," "the *Paraclete*," "the Spirit of Jesus," and "the Spirit of his Son."[65]

I suppose it would be easier to think of the Spirit as a person if the Spirit were named Tom or Sally. But those are names given

---

[64] If you think you've figured out how three can be one, without sacrificing something of their diversity or something of their unity, I can assure you that you are wrong—at least it is still a mystery of God after these past 2,000 years.

[65] This Greek word is variously translated as Comforter, Advocate, Helper, and Counselor. It is a name used often by Jesus in his last talk with his disciples. Jesus was leaving but God was sending another to be with them—the Spirit, aka the Paraclete.

by humans to other humans. The Spirit is a person, though not a human person. Don't let the seemingly impersonal nature of the word "spirit" mislead you. The Holy Spirit of God is very personal indeed.

What does the Spirit do?

Gordon Fee, the prominent Pentecostal New Testament scholar, came up with just the right phrase to describe the Spirit's work. The Spirit is the "empowering presence of God," the title of his monumental work on the Spirit in the writings of Paul. Look at the above passage from Isaiah. I've underlined a few key phrases that directly relate the *presence* of God to the Spirit of God.

Jesus does the same thing. On the night before his crucifixion, Jesus told his disciples that he was leaving, but it was okay and even better than okay, because God would send his Holy Spirit to be with them. God would still be with them, but it would be his Spirit, not Jesus. Jesus would still be with them, but it would be his Spirit.[66]

The Spirit is God with us every day. It is the Spirit who empowers and strengthens us. It is the Spirit who comforts us. It is the Spirit who lifts up to the Father the prayers that we can't even articulate ourselves. If you believe that God is helping you through a crisis, it is the Spirit who is the helper. It is the Spirit

---

[66] Yes, it takes a somewhat expansive and flexible mind to accommodate all things Trinitarian! My advice is to pay careful attention to the words of Scripture and let them guide you.

who opens people's hearts so they can hear the good news. It is the Spirit who is God-doing with us and for us every day.

It is the Holy Spirit who gathers us together for worship. Indeed, it is the Holy Spirit who has formed us into the fellowship that we call the church, the holy catholic church. And it is the Spirit who sustains us in this community of believers.

The holy, catholic church

Ok ... are we affirming somehow that all Christians are covert Roman Catholics? No. The word "catholic" simply means "universal." Thus, for example, the New Testament letters that aren't directed to any person or church in particular are sometimes referred to as the "catholic epistles" or "universal letters."

In this three word phrase, we are affirming that there is a church, the body of Christ, a universal community of believers, and that it is set apart for God, i.e., "holy." Though none of these affirmations are very controversial, it is worth exploring each of them.

The universal[67] church

Simply put, the church, aka the Body of Christ, is the worldwide community of believers, encompassing not only the living, but the believers who have died. We gather in churches to

---

[67] In the UMC hymnal, the word "universal" is rightly footnoted as an acceptable substitute for "catholic."

worship, to pray, to care for one another, and to go about the work given us by Christ. But the church is not the buildings, it is the people. The church includes believers of all the various denominations, large and small, including: United Methodist, Presbyterian, Roman Catholic, Greek Orthodox, Southern Baptist, Lutheran, the Church of Christ, and so on.

There are many images of "the church" in the Bible. It is we who are God's sheep, protected and cared for by the Good Shepherd. We are also, as Paul puts it, the body of Christ. We are his eyes and his hands and his feet in this world. We are a fellowship that was formed by God, in the person of his Holy Spirit, and is sustained by that same Spirit. Indeed, Paul refers to us as God's temple, in whom God's Spirit dwells. We are, as Peter puts it, a "chosen race, a holy nation ... God's own people." And there is only one thing that we have in common: our faith, i.e., our trust, in Jesus Christ. Faith in Jesus Christ is our one and only badge of membership, not race or gender or geography, nor our obedience to a set of rules nor our conformity to a particular set of doctrines, beyond the essentials.

A holy church

To say that God is "holy" is to say that God is, well, God. It is God who is inherently holy in himself; all other holiness is derived from God. Holiness is not an attribute of God. As Gustaf Aulen, the great Swedish theologian, put it, "holiness is the foundation on which the whole conception of God rests." Because God is just and good and righteous, because God *is* love, there is an ethical and moral dimension to holiness.

Just as we are called to be holy[68] individuals, encompassing purity, social justice, and morality, we, as the community of believers, are called to be holy. As the *Dictionary of Biblical Imagery* puts it:

> It is also possible for communities to be holy. Thus Israel is called to be a holy people (Exodus 19:6; Leviticus 19:2), meaning on the one hand that they are to be different and distinct from other peoples on the basis of their relationship with Yahweh. But there is an added ethical dimension here: there is to be a moral difference in Israel. As a holy people, Israel is to reflect the moral holiness of Yahweh its God. Similarly, members of Paul's churches are called "the saints." They are to be holy in character, and their behavior is to reflect their inspiration by the Holy Spirit.[69]

Why go to church?

It is important to address a question often posed to me. It usually goes something like this: "I believe in Jesus, but why should I have to go to church? Can't I love Jesus just as well

---

[68] Obviously, this is a holiness derived from God. Such holiness doesn't make us divine, but it does speak to making the image of God in us all shine as brilliantly as possible.

[69] Ryken, L., Wilhoit, J., Longman, T., Duriez, C., Penney, D., & Reid, D. G., *Dictionary of Biblical Imagery* (electronic ed.) (Downers Grove, Ill.: InterVarsity Press, 2000), 390.

in my living room?" I understand where the question comes from, particularly in our individualistic society.

But there is a reason that N. T. Wright writes, "It is as impossible, unnecessary, and undesirable to be a Christian all by yourself as it is to be a newborn baby all by yourself," for all those who have faith in Christ are born anew, new creations born into God's creation, the church. As another wise and informed Christian, whose name escapes me, wrote, "There is no healthy relationship with Jesus without a relationship to the church." To put it another way, we can't expect to have a healthy relationship with Jesus without a relationship with his body. And to put a finer edge on the theology, all believers are part of the body of Christ, whether they are present or absent.

You see, we humans are built for community. We are made in the image of God, who is, in his very being, inherently relational, an eternal loving fellowship of three persons: Father, Son, and Holy Spirit. Thus, it is in community with one another, believer to believer, that we discover all that God hopes for us and provides to us. It is in the midst of other believers, that we can find the meaning, the purpose, the joy, and the peace that we all seek.

Communion and forgiveness . . .

"the communion of saints, the forgiveness of sins . . .".

Psalm 103:1-5 (NRSV)

[1]Bless the LORD, O my soul,
>and all that is within me,
>bless his holy name.
[2]Bless the LORD, O my soul,
>and do not forget all his benefits—
[3]who forgives all your iniquity,
>who heals all your diseases,
[4]who redeems your life from the Pit,
>who crowns you with steadfast love and mercy,
[5]who satisfies you with good as long as you live
>so that your youth is renewed like the eagle's.

2 Corinthians 2:5-11 (NIV)

[5] If anyone has caused grief, he has not so much grieved me as he has grieved all of you to some extent—not to put it too severely. [6] The punishment inflicted on him by the majority is sufficient. [7] Now instead, you ought to forgive and comfort him, so that he will not be overwhelmed by excessive sorrow. [8] I urge you, therefore, to reaffirm your love for him. [9] Another reason I wrote you was to see if you would stand the test and be obedient in everything. [10] Anyone you forgive, I also forgive. And what I have forgiven—if

there was anything to forgive—I have forgiven in the sight of Christ for your sake, [11] in order that Satan might not outwit us. For we are not unaware of his schemes.

We continue in our affirmations about the people of God, a fellowship of forgiven sinners that has been created by the Holy Spirit.

As short as the Apostles' Creed is, there are some phrases that many of us say with little clue about what they really mean for us. One is surely "the communion of saints." So let's take a careful look at both of these important words.

Communion?

Communion translates the Greek word, *koinonia*. It is also translated "fellowship." *Koinonia* was a common Greek word, used to talk about marriage, business partnerships, politics—anywhere that people shared resources and experiences. Similarly, many churches have a room that is designated the fellowship hall. It is easy to think that fellowship is merely a warmhearted, brotherly and sisterly love. Fellowship is certainly that—but also far more. That "far more" is what we are trying to get at with the biblical idea of communion, of *koinonia*.

The best way to understand *koinonia* is to see it as "sharing in" something. At Pentecost, Jesus' followers shared in the gift and the power of the Holy Spirit, as do all Christians (2 Corinthians 13:13). Indeed, the *koinonia*, the communion, of the believers was a gift brought by the Spirit. But we also share in the Spirit, just as God has called us all to the *koinonia* of his Son, Jesus, which the apostle John makes clear in a letter to believers.

John writes: "We declare to you what we have seen and heard so that you also may have fellowship [*koinonia*/communion] with us; and truly our fellowship [*koinonia*/communion] is with the Father and with his Son Jesus Christ. We are writing these things so that our joy may be complete" (1 John 1:3-4).

Why does John want us to grasp the truth of Jesus? First, so that like the community in Jerusalem, we might have fellowship (*koinonia*) with one another (the horizontal). Second that we might have *koinonia* with the "Father and his son Jesus Christ" (the vertical). And thirdly, so that our "joy may be complete."

Saints?

Who are the saints who share this fellowship, who participate in this blessed communion? The saints are all believers, those living now, those have died, and even those who have yet to be born. The "communion of saints" is the Spirit-filled fellowship of all who have ever had or ever will have faith in Jesus Christ.

"All believers" is the meaning of "saints" whenever you come across it in the New Testament. Only later did the word come to be used for certain distinctive Christians as designated by the Roman Catholic Church.

Forgiven

It is one thing to say the words, "I am forgiven." It is another thing entirely to take it to heart. We have enough trouble forgiving ourselves or those we love the most. The idea that we will one day stand before God as a forgiven people, as a forgiven person—well, it is almost too much to comprehend. The great hymn, "Amazing Grace," is aptly named. Grace *is* amazing, even shocking. In class after class that I teach, people ask me whether forgiveness is available to the most horrid monster they can imagine, usually someone such as Hitler or a serial killer. My answer is a straightforward, "yes." Yet, no matter how many times we answer the question, "yes," it still shocks us, even scandalizes us. Could this really be, we ask?

First, ask yourself what needs forgiving. You'll find that it is all the ways in which we have failed to love God and to love one another. "Sins" is the word we often use to describe all those ways. Here is a useful definition of sin: *sin is whatever separates us from God.*

When we connecting dots, we saw that we can think of sin as a large chasm. God stands on one side of the chasm and we stand on the other side. It wasn't always this way. God once came in the evenings to walk with Adam and Eve, but that ended with their sin. They were separated from God; we are separated from God. Thus, the obvious question is how we cross the chasm to God. The short answer is that we can't cross the chasm on our own. Rather, the chasm has been closed by God, through his faithfulness to his covenant, through Jesus' faithfulness all the way to the cross.

It is God who has come to us. And it is by God's grace[70] and grace alone that we have been forgiven. In some mysterious way, never fully articulated in the New Testament, we have been reconciled to God through the death of Jesus on the cross. We have been redeemed. We have been made right with God. We have been justified. We have been forgiven. We have been saved. The chasm has been closed.

The next obvious question is this: For whom has the chasm been closed? Who has been made right with God? It is the people of God who are a forgiven people, who have been redeemed. And how would we know who those people are? The people of God are those who have faith in Jesus Christ. As the apostle Paul put it, the badge of membership in the people of God was once circumcision, keeping the Sabbath, the avoidance of pork and so on. But now, with Jesus' death and resurrection, the badge of membership in the people of God is simply faith in Jesus Christ (Romans 3:21-31).

This question quickly follows: But what about all those people who don't come to faith in Christ or have never even heard of him? Frankly, I'm glad that all this is ultimately in God's job description, not mine. Again we come back to the key question: Will we trust God? Are we really willing to rely on God's goodness, love, wisdom, mercy, and justice? I am. Do I hold out the hope that God's grace extends past the grave,

---

[70] I still like the old-fashioned definition of grace. God's grace is God's unmerited favor. If we merited (deserved) forgiveness, it wouldn't be grace. If we earned it, it isn't grace. Grace can neither be deserved nor merited or, by definition, it isn't grace.

that people might have the opportunity to come to faith in Christ after death? I do, for I can find nothing in Scripture that prevents me from genuinely holding to such hope. But in the end, I trust God.

Forgiving

The forgiven are to be forgiving. It is like breathing—in and out. We are to breathe out the very forgiveness that we have breathed in; after all, how long can any of us hold our breath. What comes in must go out—that is just how it works. This passage from 2 Corinthians is a good example.

The apostle Paul was in the business of founding communities of new Christians. We can easily imagine the problems and difficulties that must have arisen. There was a man in Corinth who must have done something terrible and was, in essence, kicked out of the Christian community. Paul was known to urge this from time to time when someone posed so big a threat that the community's existence was threatened. We don't know much about the circumstances, only what we can infer from the letter. But it's clear that Paul is telling the community the time has come to bring the man back in, to forgive and console him.

This has nothing to do with whether the man deserves the forgiveness. There is nothing said about his repentance or about a change in ways. Paul simply says it is time to forgive. Forgiveness in the New Testament "is a term whose understanding is grounded in God's giving freely and graciously to people who do not deserve it. ... [In a community] the term functions to describe the restoration of relationships between or among people."[71] Grace and forgiveness are bound together. Indeed, sometimes in the New Testament, the word translated as "forgive" (including in today's passage from 2 Corinthians) is actually a derivation from the Greek, *charis*, meaning "grace" or "gift."

Yet how hard it can be for us to offer this grace, this forgiveness, to others, even to those we love. Instead, we harbor our hurts and slights. How many spouses have not said to themselves at one time or another, "I'm not going to apologize until she apologizes first." Or perhaps, "I can't forgive until she repents."

But instead of all this counting and figuring, this balancing of hurts and slights, Jesus instructs us to simply forgive as we have been forgiven, to extend to others the grace that has been extended to us. How can we possibly do this? Only by the power of the Holy Spirit, yet another of God's many gifts. Truly, forgiveness unlocks the power of love.

---

[71] From Paul Sampley's commentary on 2 Corinthians in the *New Interpreters Bible.*

A Bit More

"Sin" and "sins"

It is worth going back over what we mean by "sin" and "sins."

By "sin," the Bible means a tragic flaw or deformity that is shared by all humans. It is something with which we all are born. It is like a beast that is always lurking, ready to consume and destroy (see the story of Cain and Abel in Genesis 4). In my classes, I often use the metaphor of a flaw in our moral DNA. It is just there and we all have it—from birth. From this flaw, from sin, springs the destruction wrought by pride, greed, jealousy, hatred, and the rest.

Where did we get this flaw? It has been with humanity almost from our beginning, when our earliest ancestors chose against God rather than for God, desiring to be like gods themselves. This is the tragic story of Adam and Eve.

But the worst consequence of all is that sin separates us from God. Adam hid from God after he rebelled against God. The biblical story is the long story of a gracious God determined to restore the relationship that we wrecked.

"A sin" or "sins" are specific transgressions of God's law, which boils down to loving God and loving neighbor.

Thus, it is sin that drives us to gossip about others, and it is a sin when we do so.

This may all seem a bit pedantic, but your Bible reading will be easier if you can differentiate between the beast called "sin" that lurks within us all and the specific sins that we commit.

Has everyone sinned? Yes, with the exception of Jesus from Nazareth; he went to his grave utterly loving God and others every minute of every day. The same can be said for no one else. Hence, our need for God's loving and gracious forgiveness revealed in the faith of Jesus Christ.

The everlasting resurrection

". . the resurrection of the body, and the life everlasting.
Amen"

1 Corinthians 15:12-24 (The Message)

Now, let me ask you something profound yet troubling. If
you became believers because you trusted the proclamation
that Christ is alive, risen from the dead, how can you let
people say that there is no such thing as a resurrection? If
there's no resurrection, there's no living Christ. And face
it—if there's no resurrection for Christ, everything we've
told you is smoke and mirrors, and everything you've staked
your life on is smoke and mirrors. Not only that, but we
would be guilty of telling a string of barefaced lies about
God, all these affidavits we passed on to you verifying
that God raised up Christ—sheer fabrications, if there's no
resurrection.

If corpses can't be raised, then Christ wasn't, because
he was indeed dead. And if Christ weren't raised, then all
you're doing is wandering about in the dark, as lost as ever.
It's even worse for those who died hoping in Christ and
resurrection, because they're already in their graves. If all we
get out of Christ is a little inspiration for a few short years,
we're a pretty sorry lot. But the truth is that Christ has been
raised up, the first in a long legacy of those who are going
to leave the cemeteries.

There is a nice symmetry in this: Death initially came by a man, and resurrection from death came by a man. Everybody dies in Adam; everybody comes alive in Christ. But we have to wait our turn: Christ is first, then those with him at his Coming, the grand consummation when, after crushing the opposition, he hands over his kingdom to God the Father.

Revelation 21:1-6 (NIV)

Then I saw "a new heaven and a new earth," for the first heaven and the first earth had passed away, and there was no longer any sea. ²I saw the Holy City, the new Jerusalem, coming down out of heaven from God, prepared as a bride beautifully dressed for her husband. ³And I heard a loud voice from the throne saying, "Look! God's dwelling place is now among the people, and he will dwell with them. They will be his people, and God himself will be with them and be their God. ⁴'He will wipe every tear from their eyes. There will be no more death' or mourning or crying or pain, for the old order of things has passed away."

⁵He who was seated on the throne said, "I am making everything new!" Then he said, "Write this down, for these words are trustworthy and true."

⁶He said to me: "It is done. I am the Alpha and the Omega, the Beginning and the End. To the thirsty I will give water without cost from the spring of the water of life."

*Alleluia! Christ is risen. And, one day,
so shall we be risen!*

And so we come to the final phrases of the Apostles' Creed. The resurrection of the body and the life everlasting are simple affirmations of the Christian hope, i.e., our confidence that the story ends well. They complete the narrative of the creed and bring us back to Jesus, for "the end" is not really about an event, but a *who*.

The resurrection of the body

Earlier in the creed we affirmed our faith that Jesus was "crucified, dead, and buried" and that "on the third day he rose from the dead." We talked about the meaning of resurrection to the ancient Jews and even the Greeks. We learned that resurrection is not the same as resuscitation, which is being brought back to life. Instead, resurrection is about moving forward from death to a newly embodied life on the other side of the grave. We can think of resurrection as death's reversal, whereas resuscitation is merely its delay.

It is important to remember that resurrection is about the restoration of the whole person—body and soul, we might say. Resurrection puts back together what death ripped apart. After his resurrection, Jesus walked with his disciples, ate with them, and even asked one to touch his wounds. He ate fish in front of them so they could see that he was still "flesh and bone" (Luke 24:36-49). Jesus' resurrected body, his flesh and bones, wasn't exactly the same as it was before, but it was similar and still quite material.

1 Corinthians 15 is a lengthy passage from Paul's letter to the believers in Corinth, Greece. They have an over-spiritualized

sense of themselves and of the Christian gospel, leading them to deny even that Jesus was actually resurrected. They thought the exalted Jesus had to be above the "messiness" of an actual material body.

Paul can hardly believe what he hears from them. Deny Jesus' resurrection!? He proceeds to list witnesses who can testify to the truth of the claim. There are nearly 500 and most are still living, Paul writes. And, he goes on, if Jesus wasn't bodily resurrected[72] then Christianity is one big lie and the believers, all those who placed their faith in Jesus, are to be pitied. "If Christ has not been raised," Paul writes, "your faith is futile and you are still in your sins ... if for this life only we have hoped in Christ, we are of all people most to be pitied" (1 Corinthians 15:17-19).

But there's more, which is the focus of the passage printed above. If Jesus wasn't resurrected, then we won't be resurrected ourselves. However, as Eugene Peterson artfully puts in his paraphrase, *The Message*, Paul writes, "the truth is that Christ has been raised up, the first in a long legacy of those who are going to leave the cemeteries. ... Everybody dies in Adam; everybody comes alive in Christ. But we have to wait our turn: Christ is first, then those with him at his Coming." To translate it more literally, Jesus Christ is "the first fruits of the those who have died." Jesus is the first to be resurrected, then

---

[72] Yes, "bodily resurrected" is redundant, but I feel compelled to say it once in awhile because I think too many Christians don't really understand the meaning of "resurrection," *anastasis* in the Greek.

when he returns, the rest of us will be resurrected too! *Full stop: The rest of us?*

Yes, simply put, the creedal affirmation, "the resurrection of the body," is not about Jesus' bodily resurrection, which we affirmed earlier in the creed, *it is about our own bodies.* As Jesus was raised so shall we all be raised! Paul puts it this way in his letter to the Romans, "If the Spirit of him who raised Jesus from the dead dwells in you, he who raised Christ from the dead will give life to your mortal bodies also through his Spirit that dwells in you" (Rom. 8:11).

The Jews of Jesus' day believed that when the last days arrived, all the dead would be resurrected. Paul is agreeing with that. Jesus is the first, and the rest of us will follow; there just happens to be 2,000 years, so far, between the first person to be resurrected, Jesus, and the rest of us. To use Paul's agricultural metaphor of Jesus as the "first fruits," God's harvest is underway, it just seems to be taking a long time, by our measure of time at least.

If this all seems just a bit too fantastical and even weird to you, consider our affirmation of Jesus' resurrection. That doesn't seem so fantastical only because we've gotten used to the idea. But once you've accepted as true the claim that Jesus was resurrected and walked out of the tomb after having died ... well, then everything is on the table. Being a Christian actually takes a big imagination, a mind and heart that refuses to try and shrink God into a small box that seems "reasonable."

Fleming Rutledge writes[73]:

> A story was told me recently that might be
> apocryphal but might well be true. The two
> people in question, both clergy, are very well
> known in the American church. One of them
> is a prolific writer of skeptical books calling
> the orthodox faith into question. The other is
> a famous preacher of the gospel. The skeptic,
> seeking to provoke the preacher, says, "My
> daughter has two Ph.D.s. How can I expect
> her to believe anything so unacceptable to
> the modern mind as the resurrection of the
> body?" The preacher says, thoughtfully, "I
> don't know your daughter. How limited is her
> imagination?"

Our belief in the resurrection of the body is the promise that I
will one day again see my grandfather—solid, material, tactile,
real. And not only see him, but hug him. What could be better
news than that?

And the life everlasting

The final affirmation is the great summing up, lifting up the
point of all this. It is the affirmation that God's great project

---

[73] From Rutledge's sermon on the resurrection of the body in *Exploring
and Proclaiming the Apostles' Creed*, Ed. Roger van Harn (Grand Rapids:
Eerdmans, 2004).

will come to its full and glorious consummation. God's will shall be done on earth as it is in heaven!

Scripture tells the story of God putting right what went wrong almost from the beginning. God created the cosmos, pronounced it good, and made humans in his image. He gave them a beautiful place to live and work. By now you understand how they threw it away, hoping to be like gods themselves. So God set about to put things right. God chose a people, Abraham and his descendants, through whom this restoration would proceed. In the end, God, in the person of Jesus Christ, would have to do for Israel and all humanity what they were—and we still are—unable to do for ourselves: simply love God and love neighbor.

When we affirm our belief in everlasting life, it is certainly about ourselves, but it is also about much more. God's renewal of creation and the restoration of loving relationship is what it has always been about. They are the fulfillment of promises God made through his prophets.

All will be well

It is so easy to be caught up in the troubles and terrors of our lives and our world. Too often, we are overwhelmed by our anxieties and fears. Yet, the Bible's promise of a day with no death or tears or pain is God's assurance that all will be well. John Ortberg wrote recently of our hunger for joy, rightful hunger because joy lies at the core of the cosmos. We may not always know that all will be well, but God knows it. Ortberg quotes a Christian who lived long ago, Julian of Norwich:

> "All will be well,
> And all will be well,
> And in all manner of things, all will be well."

All this we proclaim each time we stand and affirm the Apostles' Creed. Each phrase of the creed is packed with meaning and good news. For nearly 2,000 years, we believers have stood together to announce with one voice these most basic of truths.

Part 3

---•---

Confronting the Objections

Unearthing our core convictions

The Really Hard Questions

Given the rise of the so-called "new atheists," such as Christopher Hitchens and Richard Dawkins, such questions have been getting more press than usual. And as with all things Christian, the discussions are too often built upon misunderstandings and mistakes.

And even amongst us Christians, certain questions get to the heart of what we really believe about our world, about God, and about ourselves. Yet, we often get off on the wrong foot. What is it that we believe? Why do we believe it? What do we mean by "believe?" A simple intellectual affirmation or a deeply held conviction?

In this passage,[74] evangelical California pastor John Ortberg points us to Catholic philosopher Michael Novak's description of three different kinds of convictions: public, private, and core.

> Public convictions are those beliefs that we try to get other people to think we believe whether or not we really do. It is what happens when politicians say, 'This is the greatest nation on earth,' when in reality they are not sure. Private convictions are more subtle. These are

---

[74] From Ortberg's review of Dallas Willard's *Knowing Christ Today: Why We Can Trust Spiritual Knowledge* (San Francisco: HarperOne, 2009):

beliefs that I may *think* I hold in the abstract, but when circumstances allow them to be tested it turns out that I don't really believe them. For instance, when I am in church listening to a sermon I may think I believe, "it is more blessed to give than to receive;" I give mental and emotional assent to it, but when I look at the way I live, it becomes clear I do not actually believe this.

Core convictions, then, are what Dallas would call our ideas about the way things really are,[75] and he notes that we always live at the mercy of these ideas. I cannot violate, for example, my belief in the law of gravity. My actions are always a result of my purposes and my convictions about the way things really are. … Our public convictions may be bogus, our private convictions may be fickle, but our lives will always reflect our core convictions.

Ortberg's larger point is that churches settle for shaping members' private convictions, rarely helping them to unearth and transform their core convictions. Hence, discipleship programs languish and even worship attendance becomes

---

[75] This is what people mean when they refer to a "worldview." Your worldview provides your answers to the most important questions about life. Everyone has a worldview, whether they give it much thought or can articulate it. Have you ever gotten in an argument that seemed to go on and on until someone says, "That's just how things are!" Well, you've run right into their worldview.

optional. Get any group of church leaders together, and they'll tell you how difficult it is to help people become more genuine disciples of Jesus Christ. Rarely, however, will those leaders diagnose the problem as well as Ortberg and Willard.

This final part of the book gets at those core convictions. I'll at least try to help you unearth some of your core convictions, and, perhaps, I can help you begin to challenge them. When Paul urges believers to "be transformed by the renewing of your minds" (Romans 12:2), this reshaping of core convictions is exactly what he means.

Here's the six questions that we are going to tackle. As you'll see, each one gets at core convictions that shape our response to God, as well as our life with God and one another:

- Why does God seem to play hide-and-seek?
- Why does God allow evil in the world?
- Why is Jesus the only way to God?
- Why do so many Christians give Christianity a bad name?
- Why does God look so much like a bully in the Old Testament?
- Why does Christianity include a hell?

There are three foundational principles in how we'll go about this. First, we'll work from the belief that there is a God who reveals himself in his actions and in Scripture. Second, we'll work from the historically grounded belief that Jesus of Nazareth was resurrected by God in Jerusalem on a spring morning in about AD 30, after having been crucified by the

Romans. Third, we'll work from the belief that Scripture is the inspired word of God, written through humans and uniquely "God-breathed."

So, with all that, let's get started.

God, Where Are You?

Exodus 33:12-16 (NIV)

[12] Moses said to the LORD, "You have been telling me, 'Lead these people,' but you have not let me know whom you will send with me. You have said, 'I know you by name and you have found favor with me.' [13] If you are pleased with me, teach me your ways so I may know you and continue to find favor with you. Remember that this nation is your people."

[14] The LORD replied, "My Presence will go with you, and I will give you rest."

[15] Then Moses said to him, "If your Presence does not go with us, do not send us up from here. [16] How will anyone know that you are pleased with me and with your people unless you go with us? What else will distinguish me and your people from all the other people on the face of the earth?"

Psalm 139 (NRSV)

[1] O LORD, you have searched me and known me.
    [2] You know when I sit down and when I rise up;
        you discern my thoughts from far away.
    [3] You search out my path and my lying down,
        and are acquainted with all my ways.
    [4] Even before a word is on my tongue,
    O LORD, you know it completely.
    [5] You hem me in, behind and before,

and lay your hand upon me.
⁶Such knowledge is too wonderful for me;
    it is so high that I cannot attain it.
⁷Where can I go from your spirit?
Or where can I flee from your presence?
⁸If I ascend to heaven, you are there;
    if I make my bed in Sheol, you are there.
⁹If I take the wings of the morning
    and settle at the farthest limits of the sea,
¹⁰even there your hand shall lead me,
    and your right hand shall hold me fast.
¹¹If I say, "Surely the darkness shall cover me,
    and the light around me become night,"
¹²even the darkness is not dark to you;
    the night is as bright as the day,
    for darkness is as light to you.

Too often, it seems as if God is playing hide-and-seek with us, particularly when we are really hurting. We feel lost and very alone. But does God go somewhere? Is God really hiding? How can we be confident of God's presence?

The hide-and-seek God?

A student in one of my classes once came to me with a question. He began it this way: "I know, of course, that God created everything, is letting things run forward and isn't involved in the day-to-day, but here's my question ...." N. T. Wright tells the story of a student who came to him to say that he didn't believe in God. When Wright asked him to describe God, the student said, "You know, the god[76] who doesn't get involved in the daily muck of our lives, but keeps a list of what we do wrong." Wright replied, "Well, I don't believe in that god either."

In both cases, we're seeing the students' core convictions—that there may be a god, but this god is pretty much an absentee landlord, who created the universe but stays out of the picture except, perhaps, on those rare occasions when this god intervenes in what we call a "miracle."

Sadly, I think that God as the Absentee Landlord is a core conviction held by many Christians. They may not articulate it in that way, but they just don't see God as being involved in our daily lives. Instead, God is a superhero who shows up once in awhile. Why sometimes and not others? Who knows? The truth is this was once among my core convictions. Christianity was about stuff that happened in the past and a set of beliefs I affirmed, but not the reality of an ever-present, ever-caring, ever-loving, ever-faithful, ever-personal, ever-relational God.

But when I began to take Scripture seriously, really listening to some wise teachers, I began to see just how wrong I had been. "Absentee" is the last label you'd pin on God based on even a cursory reading of Scripture. God is everywhere and deeply involved. This is why I am such an advocate of regular Bible reading, study, and engagement. If all we work from is our own

---

[76] You've probably noticed that in my writing, I reserve the capitalized "God" for the God revealed in Scripture. All the other "gods" get lowercase treatment. I find this to be a clarifying practice.

feelings, what we learned in Sunday School as a youngster, and what can be gleaned from the latest History Channel special, we will never dislodge the mistaken core convictions that lurk in our minds and hearts, including the one about the Absentee Landlord.[77]

Take the story of the Exodus for example. God leads his people out of Egypt. God is present with them in a way that God has not been present with any other people. God is present in the pillar of fire that leads them through the wilderness. God is present with them in the clouds that settle on the top of Mount Sinai. Moses ascends the mountain to talk with God, as he had spoken with God at the burning bush.

During Moses' absence, the people make a religious idol, a golden calf, and begin to worship the hunk of gold, giving it credit for rescuing them from Pharaoh. The above excerpt from Exodus 33 is part of the conversations between God and Moses. God has told Moses that God can no longer be present with his people as he had been. But Moses tells God that he must remain with them, present with them. And God relents. God will remain with his people. God's dwelling place will be inside the tabernacle the people will build, and there Moses will be able to talk with God.

God's empowering presence is a major theme throughout the Old Testament. There is even a Hebrew word, *shekinah*, for

---

[77] For those more familiar with the jargon of theology, the Absentee Landlord is pretty much a synonym for Deism, the belief system of some of our founding fathers, including Benjamin Franklin and Thomas Jefferson.

God's presence, though "spirit" and "wisdom" are also images of the God-Who-Is-Present. ... Never absent, always present.

This same God is present with us now. Just as the psalmist knows that there is no escaping God, "Where can I go from your spirit? Or where can I flee from your presence?," so God is present with us now.

We talk much of the Holy Spirit in church, but, sadly, I think the Spirit is absent from many Christians' core convictions. They don't grasp that the Spirit is simply the God-Who-Is-Present; that's who the Spirit is. God involved in all the daily muck of our lives, in ways seen and unseen. The Spirit is both the evidence that the kingdom of God, promised by Jesus (Mark 1:15) at the beginning of his public ministry, has arrived and the guarantee that God will bring his work in this world to its glorious conclusion.

The Spirit as evidence[78]

To go back over a bit of ground, the Holy Spirit (aka "the Spirit," "the Spirit of God," "the Spirit of Christ") is not a *what* but a *who*. The Spirit is God. Not the Father and not the Son, but still God. Fully and completely God though not all of God. The Spirit is every bit as personal and genuine and God as Jesus is personal and genuine and God. In Acts, we are told about

---

[78] It is biblical scholar and theologian Gordon Fee who introduced me to this notion of evidence and guarantee. There is a fuller explanation in his book, *Paul, the Spirit, and the People of God*, published now by Baker Books.

people who lie to the Spirit (Acts 5). Who lies to electricity or even to their dog? We lie to other persons.

Paul refers to Jesus as the "first fruits of those who have died" (1 Corinthians 15:20). Likewise, the followers of Jesus are the "first fruits of the Spirit" (Romans 8:23). "First fruits" is an agricultural metaphor referring to the beginning of the harvest. Both Jesus' resurrection and the arrival[79] of the Spirit marked the coming of God's kingdom, which has arrived already but has "not yet" been consummated.[80]

Like Jesus' resurrection, the arrival of the Spirit during the festival of Pentecost was direct evidence that God's new age had dawned. Likewise, Paul's own experience of the Spirit and the experiences of other Christians was evidence that in Christ's life, death, and resurrection, God's work had come to its climax.

The Spirit as guarantee

Though Jesus' resurrection and the arrival of the Spirit are the first fruits of God's harvest, we want to know when it is all

---

[79] Huh? Did God go somewhere? Not long before the destruction of the temple, God's dwelling place, in 586BC, the prophet Ezekiel has a vision of God's presence leaving the temple. After all, how could the Babylonians destroy the temple in Jerusalem if God were still present there? The New Testament writers' perspective is that God's Spirit returned to his people after Jesus' resurrection and ascension, on the day of Pentecost (Acts 2). And, indeed, God returned to the temple, only now the temple is (1) the church, the body of Christ and (2) individual believers.

[80] For more on the already/not yet reality of the kingdom of God, see the explanation at the end of Part 1.

going to be consummated. When will suffering, sickness, sin, and tragedy be swept away? Paul is no fool. He knows that there is much wrong in the world. But he sees the Spirit as the guarantee that all will be put right—that, not only will God's victory be won, it *has* been won!

Paul writes, "When you believed you were marked in him with a seal, the promised Holy Spirit, who is a deposit guaranteeing our inheritance ..." (Ephesians 1:13-14 (NIV). Again, "And do not grieve the Holy Spirit of God, with whom you were sealed for the day of redemption" (Ephesians 4:30, NIV). And, "But it is God who establishes us with you in Christ and has anointed us, by putting his seal on us and giving us his Spirit in our hearts as a first installment (2 Corinthians 1:21-22, NRSV)."

In the ancient world, letters were sent on a piece of rolled up papyrus that would often be marked with the seal of the sender. If the sender's seal arrived intact, then the recipient could be sure of the sender and confident that no one had tampered with the letter. The Holy Spirit, who is God's gift to everyone who has faith in Jesus, is God's seal on each of his people, marking us out as belonging to God. But the Spirit is more than a seal. The Spirit is a down payment, a first installment on all of God's promises. It is a bit like the old lay-away plan. The store would hold the merchandise as payments were made, guaranteeing that the item would one day belong the customer.

The experience of Pentecost was not limited to the disciples gathered in Jerusalem. Every Christian experiences a Pentecost of his or her own, for all Christians are empowered by the Spirit of God. Some Christians have a very powerful experience of the Holy Spirit while, for others, it is a quiet experience. But the Holy Spirit seals us *all* for God.

God never hides

Our feelings can fool us. We all feel separated from God from time to time. Indeed, such feelings can linger for long periods. We wonder where God has gone, why he isn't listening to us, why our prayers seem to go unanswered.

This is where those core convictions come into play. If your core convictions are grounded upon a god who is an absentee landlord, then, of course, you'll be convinced that just when you need him most, God is nowhere to be found. He'd just be absent, leaving you to make your own way forward as best you can, leaving you to be the master of your fate and the captain of your soul.

But if your core convictions are grounded upon the God whose ever-presence is revealed by his actions with real people in this very real world, as told in Scripture, then you can move through the sense of separation confident that God hasn't gone anywhere. If anything, you're the one who's drifted. Trust me, it makes all the difference.

Being confident that God is always present with you, in the person of his Holy Spirit, doesn't mean that all will go as you hoped or that all your prayers will be answered in the way that you want. But it does mean that you are never alone, that nothing can separate you from God. As Paul wrote to the Christians in Rome: "For I am convinced that neither death, nor life, nor angels, nor rulers, nor things present, nor things to come, nor powers, nor height, nor depth, nor anything else in all creation, will be able to separate us from the love of God in Christ Jesus our Lord" (Romans 8:38-39).

And the love of which Paul speaks is not some sort of distant affection from a remote god, but the active, caring, faithful, in-the-daily-muck love of God. If you were to say to Paul, "But I just don't feel loved," I'm confident his reply would be along these lines: "But you are loved, you are loved, you are loved. Look at that cross. That's real love. On it hung the God who loves you and is never apart from you."

What About Evil?

Genesis 1:27-28, 31 (NIV)

²⁷ So God created mankind in his own image,

in the image of God he created them;

male and female he created them.

²⁸ God blessed them and said to them, "Be fruitful and increase in number; fill the earth and subdue it. Rule over the fish in the sea and the birds in the sky and over every living creature that moves on the ground."

³¹ God saw all that he had made, and it was very good. And there was evening, and there was morning—the sixth day.

Job 4:1-2, 7-8; 38:1-4; 40:1-2 (NIV)

[After Job has lost everything his friends come to sit with him in silence for seven days. Then they make the mistake of opening their mouths.]

Then Eliphaz the Temanite replied:

² "If someone ventures a word with you, will you be impatient?

But who can keep from speaking?

⁷ "Consider now: Who, being innocent, has ever perished?

Where were the upright ever destroyed?

⁸ As I have observed, those who plow evil

and those who sow trouble reap it.

[After long discussions of all the possible reasons for Job's suffering, God arrives with a word of his own.]

Then the LORD spoke to Job out of the storm. He said:

> ² "Who is this that obscures my plans
>> with words without knowledge?
>> ³ Brace yourself like a man;
>> I will question you,
>> and you shall answer me.
>> ⁴ "Where were you when I laid the earth's foundation?
>> Tell me, if you understand.

The LORD said to Job:

> ² "Will the one who contends with the Almighty correct him?
>> Let him who accuses God answer him!"

Romans 8:18-25 (NIV)

¹⁸ I consider that our present sufferings are not worth comparing with the glory that will be revealed in us. ¹⁹ For the creation waits in eager expectation for the children of God to be revealed. ²⁰ For the creation was subjected to frustration, not by its own choice, but by the will of the one who subjected it, in hope ²¹ that the creation itself will be liberated from its bondage to decay and brought into the freedom and glory of the children of God.

²² We know that the whole creation has been groaning as in the pains of childbirth right up to the present time. ²³ Not only so,

but we ourselves, who have the firstfruits of the Spirit, groan inwardly as we wait eagerly for our adoption to sonship, the redemption of our bodies. [24] For in this hope we were saved. But hope that is seen is no hope at all. Who hopes for what they already have? [25] But if we hope for what we do not yet have, we wait for it patiently.

Could there really be an all-powerful, all-good God when this world is filled with so much tragedy and suffering? Why doesn't God do something about it?!

The apparent contradiction in the coexistence of evil and a good God is the most common challenge thrown at Christians by skeptics. Historically, it has been the most persistent argument against the existence of the God revealed in Scripture and proclaimed by his followers.

This isn't hard to understand. Look around. Pick up a newspaper. Check the internet. Turn on a TV. Wherever we turn we are bombarded by images of evil and wrong inflicted on innocent people. Where does it all come from? How could so much be wrong in a world supposedly created and cared for by an all-powerful, all-good deity? Perhaps this deity isn't powerful enough to do something about it. Or perhaps this deity isn't really as good as we think he is.

You get the picture. First, understand that this is only a problem for monotheistic religions. If you believe there are many gods, then the wrongs are simply inflicted by one or another of the lesser deities. In fact, you might live your life mostly trying to stay out of their way, as many of the ancient peoples did. In a polytheistic religion, there is no single all-powerful, all-good deity whom you could accuse.

And if you are basically a pantheist (everything is divine), then the many wrongs are simply just how things are. There is no one at whom you could point your finger in blame. In fact, you might even believe that all this good and evil stuff is just an illusion.

If you are a gnostic, then this world was made by a second-rate sort of god who botched the job. Hardly the picture of an all-powerful, all-good god. Such a bumbling deity needs our pity, not our accusations.

The "problem of evil," as it is often called, is a problem only for those who believe that there is only one god, who made everything there is. Hence, it is a "problem" only for Christians, Jews, and Muslims.

Before we go further, let's talk about the meaning of "evil." Webster's is helpful here. "Evil" is defined as "morally reprehensible" and "the fact of suffering misfortune." These are often referred to as "moral evil" and "natural evil." Moral evil consists of the many wrongs we humans inflict on one another. Natural evil is the suffering inflicted by natural forces such as hurricanes, earthquakes, disease, and so on. Humans have the power to lessen the damage and suffering that goes with such events, but we don't inflict them on one another, or at least not most of the time.

Starting at the beginning

I included the passage from Genesis because it is the place where the problem of evil first arises. God created everything there is. Everything. Before God created, there was nothing. God didn't need any raw materials or a place to begin. God simply created.

And God pronounces his creation as good. Every last bit of it. Every corner. Just as God is good, so is his creation.

So where does evil come from? After all, it surely exists, doesn't it? We see evidence of moral and natural evil every day. So if God created everything, didn't God create evil as well? Yet, God surely *can't* be the author of evil if God is truly good and loving.

Hence, Christian theologians have always been careful to say that "evil" is not created. Evil is not a "thing" like a chair or even kindness. Evil is simply nothingness. Evil is the absence of the good, in much the same way that darkness is the absence of light and cold is the absence of heat. Referring to "evil" is a way of referring to the absence of the good. Evil can never create anything; it can only destroy.

But could evil be destroyed? Since evil hasn't been created, we can speak of its "destruction" in this way. Evil is destroyed when the good is enlarged. Think of it like turning on a lamp. The darkness is banished—it is simply no longer dark. Like evil, darkness isn't really created, it is the absence of light. More light = less darkness. More good = less evil.

So, what is the origin for all the evil acts we perpetrate on one another, the moral evil that rages across the planet? The biblical answer is that they originate in our free will. The biblical claim is that God created us in his image with the free will to do what is good or to do what is not good, i.e., what is evil. You and I make a myriad of these choices every day, some big and some seemingly so small that they go unnoticed. Do we act out of the interest of others (that's good) or our own interests (not so good)? Are we generous (good) or stingy (not good)? Admittedly, we usually reserve the word "evil" for the big stuff and almost always for the wrongs done by others. But if we understand that evil is the lessening of what is good, than we can begin to understand that whether we are talking about "wrongs" or "injustice" or "evil," we are talking about those acts that diminish goodness.

But what about so-called "natural evil" and all the suffering that goes with hurricanes and such? Here, we come to a pretty astonishing biblical claim. There is a wildness to creation in the Genesis account of creation. It is a creation that is dynamic and needs to be tamed. Then, in the passage from Romans 8, Paul says that all creation is in bondage, awaiting its own redemption, creation is in labor pains, waiting for the day when all will be put right. Thus, in the biblical view it isn't just we humans who need to be transformed so that we can love God and neighbor, but all the cosmos awaits its own renewal and restoration. Profound indeed were the consequences of humanity's rebellion against God.

But ...

All that said, we still rage at the suffering and injustices that surround us. There is something profoundly wrong with a world in which a child gets cancer. Philosophies and theologies don't really get us very far. We look to God and ask why. Why don't you do something about this? Why don't you save this little girl?!

Many people mistakenly think that the book of Job provides answers they seek. Job is a good man who loses everything because of a wager between God and Satan. He wants answers as to why all the terrible things have happened to him and his family. But he gets none. When God arrives on the scene, it is simply to remind Job that God is God and Job is not. Who is he to demand answers of his creator?

In the end, the story of a Job is a story of trust and faith. Will Job trust in God even in the midst of his suffering and pain? It is the same question you and I face. Will we trust God even in the face of our own suffering and unanswerable questions? Will we trust God's promises that, in the end, we will enjoy a renewed and transformed world free from tragedy, illness, suffering, and death? Will we trust that God is all-powerful and all-loving even though, at times, it doesn't seem possible to us?

The God-Who-Suffers

Like so much else in our admittedly odd Christian proclamation to the world, all these questions come to Jesus on that cross.

We proclaim that Jesus is God incarnate. But how often do we stop to contemplate that this God whom we proclaim really and truly suffered, just as the rest of humanity suffered? Or that his mother suffered as she stood at the foot of the cross and watched her tortured son die a humiliating death? Or that his Father suffered as his only begotten Son met the worst that fallen humanity has to offer? That the One through whom, in whom, and for whom all things were created ... yes, that One suffered and died.

We throw our accusations at God, failing to grasp that God has already received the worst from us. Bishop Wright puts it this way:

> The Gospels thus tell the story, unique in the world's great literature, religious theories, and philosophies: the story of the creator God taking responsibility for what's happened to creation, bearing the weight of its problems on his own shoulders. As Sydney Carter put it in one of his finest songs, 'It's God they ought to crucify, instead of you and me.' Or, as one old evangelistic tract put it, the nations of the world got together to pronounce sentence on God for all the evils in the world, only to realize with a shock that God had already served his sentence.... The tidal wave of evil crashed over the head of God himself. The spear went into his side like a plane crashing into a great building. God has been there. He has taken the weight of the world's evil on his own shoulders. This

is not an explanation. It is not a philosophical conclusion. It is an event in which, as we gaze on in horror, we may perhaps glimpse God's presence in the deepest darkness of our world, God's strange unlooked-for victory over the evil of our world; and then, and only then, may glimpse also God's vocation to us to work with him on the new solution to the new problem of evil.[81]

Jesus' own suffering shows us the incomprehensible extent of God's love for each of us. "God so loved the world that he gave his only Son...." Let's be clear about one thing: There is no one for whom I would allow one of my own sons to be crucified. I am simply not capable of loving as God loves. In contrast, even in the most terrible circumstances of our lives, it is God's concrete love expressed in Jesus' suffering that grounds our worth.

Each of us is defined by God's love for us. It is God's love, and our knowing that we are loved, that not only sustains us through suffering but enables us to put it behind us, always pressing forward to the future. Just as Jesus' crucifixion is the concrete expression of God's love for us, Jesus' resurrection is the concrete affirmation, indeed fulfillment, of our own eventual freedom from evil and suffering.

---

[81] From Wright's book, *Evil and the Justice of God* (Downers Grove, Ill.: InterVarsity Press, 2006).

The question for us is the same question that Job had to face. Will we trust this God, this strange and unexpected God-Who-Suffers, with all our questions and our hurt and our anger?

Is Jesus Really the Only Way?

John 14:1-7 (NIV)

"Do not let your hearts be troubled. You believe in God; believe also in me. ² My Father's house has many rooms; if that were not so, would I have told you that I am going there to prepare a place for you? ³ And if I go and prepare a place for you, I will come back and take you to be with me that you also may be where I am. ⁴ You know the way to the place where I am going."

⁵ Thomas said to him, "Lord, we don't know where you are going, so how can we know the way?"

⁶ Jesus answered, "I am the way and the truth and the life. No one comes to the Father except through me. ⁷ If you really know me, you will know my Father as well. From now on, you do know him and have seen him."

Colossians 1:15-20 (NRSV)

¹⁵He is the image of the invisible God,
the firstborn of all creation;
¹⁶for in him all things in heaven and on earth were created,
things visible and invisible,
whether thrones or dominions or rulers or powers
all things have been created through him and for him.
¹⁷He himself is before all things,
and in him all things hold together.

¹⁸He is the head of the body, the church;

>He is the beginning,

>>the firstborn from the dead,

>>so that he might come to have first place in
>>>everything.

¹⁹For in him all the fullness of God was pleased to dwell,

²⁰and through him God was pleased to reconcile to himself
>all things,

>>whether on earth or in heaven,

>>by making peace through the blood of his cross.

Few Christian claims fall harder on the nonbelieving ear in our culture than the claim that Jesus, and only Jesus, is the way to God. Indeed, not merely a path to God, but God himself.

"I am the way and the truth and the life. No one comes to the Father except through me. If you really know me, you will know my Father as well. From now on, you do know him and have seen him" (John 14:6-7). There you have it. Could Jesus be any more clear? Ask any of Jesus' fellow Jews on the streets of Jerusalem who the Father is and you'd have gotten a straightforward response: "The Lord God Almighty, of course, the God of Abraham, Isaac, and Jacob, the God who revealed himself to Moses at the burning bush and led us out of slavery in Egypt. That's who the Father is." And, of course, the next words out of their mouth would be astonishment and shock at the words coming out of Jesus' mouth.

Earlier, Jesus had asserted, "I am one with the Father" (John 10:30). Now, Jesus has claimed that if you have seen Jesus, you have seen the Father. That Jesus is *the* way, *the* truth, *the* life. Gail O'Day rightly notes that "these verses announce in clear language the theological conviction that drives the Fourth Evangelist's work. ... These words express the Fourth Evangelist's unshakeable belief that the coming of Jesus, the Word made flesh, decisively altered the relationship between God and humanity."[82] As the Evangelist put it when he opened his gospel: "In the beginning was the Word, and the Word was with God, and the Word was God."

From the beginning, Jesus' followers struggled to come to grips with his claims. Who can forgive sins but God!? Jesus can (Mark 2:5). It is no wonder that some people thought he was crazy (Mark 3:20-27) and others thought him blasphemous (John 10:31-33). Later, after Jesus' death and resurrection, his followers struggled to clarify their claims about Jesus. One example is the Christ-hymn of Colossians.

The Christ-hymn

Colossians 1:15-20 is a bit like a hymn in two stanzas, v. 15-17 and v. 18-20. I've printed it in verse form to help you see its poetry and structure.[83]

---

[82] From Gail O'Day's commentary on the Gospel of John in *The New Interpreter's Bible*, p. 743.

[83] Even within Paul's letters, there are still older hymns and creedlike passages. The "Christ Hymn" of Phil. 2:6-11 is one and is presented in poetic form in most translations. In 1 Cor. 11:23-26, Paul explicitly passes on the tradition about the Lord's supper that was given to him by others. And in Colossians 1:15-20, we have another of Paul's hymns. Its language and structure suggest that Paul has incorporated an early Christian hymn.

The first stanza emphasizes that all things were created in Christ, through Christ, and for Christ. In case we miss Paul's point here, he gives us a list: all things visible and invisible, all thrones, dominions, rulers, and powers. Eugene Peterson paraphrases Paul this way in *The Message*:

> We look at this Son and see the God who cannot be seen. We look at this Son and see God's original purpose in everything created. For everything, absolutely everything, above and below, visible and invisible, rank after rank after rank of angels—*everything* got started in him and finds its purpose in him. He was there before any of it came into existence and holds it all together right up to this moment.

For any Jew, this sort of language could be used only with respect to the Lord God. Paul was a Jew and not just any Jew, but an educated, zealous Pharisee. He knew the meaning of what he wrote. He knew that he was speaking of Jesus as one would speak of God. Yes, Paul struggles to find the right language, just as Christians have been struggling for 2,000 years to make sense of a mystery. On the one hand, Paul says that Jesus is the "firstborn of all creation" which might make us think he is about to lump Jesus in with the rest of creation. But no. In the next phrase, Paul says the opposite—all things are created in, through, and for Jesus!

We can be sure of the passage's power, which is easier to appreciate when written out as a poem. I urge you to read it aloud as a poem and a proclamation of the supremacy of Christ.

It takes an expansive, open, and imaginative mind to hold together seemingly contradictory truths about God. Such minds are God's desire for us.

Notice also that Paul speaks of *all* things and *all* powers. There is no person, no government, no angel, no demon—nothing— that was not created in, through, and for Jesus. Everyone, everywhere, at all times, sits under the lordship of Jesus Christ, whether or not they know or acknowledge it.

The focus of the second stanza shifts from creation to re-creation, renewal, and restoration, the embodiment of which is the church. Christ is head of the church, yet distinct from it, just as Christ is distinct from creation. Why is Jesus Christ, though fully and completely human, unique? Because he is the one person in whom God's fullness[84] dwells.

And what is God's purpose in all this? The reconciliation of the entire cosmos to God, the undoing of the tragedy of the garden. And how is all this done? Through the crucifixion, the "blood of his cross." This is the good in Good Friday—that, in a way we cannot fully explain, we and the entire cosmos have been put right with God through Jesus' death on the cross. To some, such a claim is not only bizarre but offensive, but for almost 2,000 years, Christians have proclaimed that it is true.

---

[84] Peterson is very helpful when paraphrasing "For in him all the fullness of God was pleased to dwell." From *The Message*: "So spacious is he, so roomy, that everything of God finds its proper place in him without crowding."

The only way?

I've probably belabored the point about Jesus' deity. But it is essential to understand the Christian claim. Jesus is the way, the truth, and the life. Seeing him is seeing God. Our irreducible claim is that he is God. And if we are right about this, then, of course, how could one claim to know God and yet deny Jesus? He is not merely one of the great prophets. He is not merely a great teacher and rabbi. He didn't come merely to show us a better way of living nor merely to be an example of sacrificial love. Jesus is the incarnation of the one true God, the God of Abraham and of Moses. Jesus has revealed much to us about God that we would not know without Jesus.

With all this, Christians today are left with only a few choices:

We could simply shut up and enjoy our own private relationship with Jesus. But, then, how could we ever do as Jesus instructed us: "Go and make disciples of all nations, baptizing them in the name of the Father, the Son, and the Holy Spirit" (Matthew 28:19). No, the Christian proclamation of the good news is meant for the whole world. Shutting up isn't really an option.

We could change our claims about Jesus to make him more "acceptable" to non-believers. Let's just see if we can't discover a Jesus who is deeply spiritual, but no more than a poor, Galilean itinerant preacher. It really isn't that hard to construct a Jesus to anyone's liking. Of course, it wouldn't really be Jesus, but at least we'd all just get along.

Or, we could learn what it is we Christians have claimed about Jesus for most of the last two millennia and then state it boldly and lovingly to all who would hear. The good news is not exclusionary; it is a joyous proclamation that God has rescued and is rescuing all humanity and all creation.

Our truth claim about Jesus is far too unique to fit with other belief systems. He is not merely a path to God; he is God! Could we be wrong about this? Of course. But I believe with all my mind and heart that we are not. I believe that Jesus the Galilean was truly resurrected on that Sunday morning nearly 2,000 years ago, and that belief changes everything.

One caution before closing. Nothing here allows for any sense of superiority on the part of those who have come to faith in Christ. Knowing him is a gift from God, pure and simple.

I share with you a meditation on Jesus as the way, the truth, and the life written more than five centuries ago by Thomas à Kempis:

Follow thou me, I am the way and the truth and the life.
Without the way there is no going;
without the truth there is no knowing;
without the life there is no living.
I am the way which thou must follow;
the truth which thou must believe;
the life for which thou must hope.
I am the inviolable way; the infallible truth;
the never ending life.

I am the straightest way; the sovereign truth; life true, life
blessed, life uncreated.
If thou remain in my way thou shalt know the truth,
and the truth shall make thee free,
and thou shalt lay hold on eternal life.

Real Christians?

John 3:1-10, 16 (NIV)

Now there was a Pharisee, a man named Nicodemus who was a member of the Jewish ruling council. [2] He came to Jesus at night and said, "Rabbi, we know that you are a teacher who has come from God. For no one could perform the signs you are doing if God were not with him."

[3] Jesus replied, "Very truly I tell you, no one can see the kingdom of God unless they are born again."

[4] "How can someone be born when they are old?" Nicodemus asked. "Surely they cannot enter a second time into their mother's womb to be born!"

[5] Jesus answered, "Very truly I tell you, no one can enter the kingdom of God unless they are born of water and the Spirit. [6] Flesh gives birth to flesh, but the Spirit gives birth to spirit. [7] You should not be surprised at my saying, 'You must be born again.' [8] The wind blows wherever it pleases. You hear its sound, but you cannot tell where it comes from or where it is going. So it is with everyone born of the Spirit."

[9] "How can this be?" Nicodemus asked.

[10] "You are Israel's teacher," said Jesus, "and do you not understand these things?

[16] For God so loved the world that he gave his one and only Son, that whoever believes in him shall not perish but have eternal life.

Colossians 3:1-14 (NIV)

Since, then, you have been raised with Christ, set your hearts on things above, where Christ is, seated at the right hand of God. [2] Set your minds on things above, not on earthly things. [3] For you died, and your life is now hidden with Christ in God. [4] When Christ, who is your life, appears, then you also will appear with him in glory.

[5] Put to death, therefore, whatever belongs to your earthly nature: sexual immorality, impurity, lust, evil desires and greed, which is idolatry. [6] Because of these, the wrath of God is coming. [7] You used to walk in these ways, in the life you once lived. [8] But now you must also rid yourselves of all such things as these: anger, rage, malice, slander, and filthy language from your lips. [9] Do not lie to each other, since you have taken off your old self with its practices [10] and have put on the new self, which is being renewed in knowledge in the image of its Creator. [11] Here there is no Gentile or Jew, circumcised or uncircumcised, barbarian, Scythian, slave or free, but Christ is all, and is in all.

[12] Therefore, as God's chosen people, holy and dearly loved, clothe yourselves with compassion, kindness, humility, gentleness and patience. [13] Bear with each other and forgive one another if any of you has a grievance against someone. Forgive as the Lord forgave you. [14] And over all these virtues put on love, which binds them all together in perfect unity.

It bothers me that so many Christians give Christianity a bad name. It plays into the hands of those who are looking for an excuse

*to ignore us. What does it really mean to be a Christian,
and what responsibilities come with it?*

"I don't go to church. They are all just a bunch of hypocrites."
How many times have you heard something like that? Too
many to count, I'd bet.

First, hypocrisy is pretending to be what one is not, especially
when it comes to virtues and religion. I'll grant that there are
probably genuine hypocrites in church, but for many Christians
striving to be better disciples of Jesus, their mistakes are not
hypocrisy but simply a failure to yet be the person they are
striving to be. A high jumper who is trying to clear seven
feet and failing isn't a hypocrite, just an athlete trying to get
better.

Nonetheless, it is hard to deny that there are many who proclaim
themselves Christian but are a terrible witness to Christ. Some
are very public about it. Here, I'm thinking of men like Robert
Tilton, Jim Bakker, and others. Some of these very public
embarrassments are simply disciples caught up in the glittering
vices. Others, I fear, are frauds. Blessedly, in the end, only God
can know the true state of anyone's heart.

And then there are well-meaning Christians who say the most
stupid and hateful things that are anything but a testimony
to the love of God and the good news. As someone who says
and writes thousands of public words each week, I am well
aware of the dangers and am the first to ask for grace and the
benefit of the doubt from time to time. Nonetheless, I wish
some Christian leaders would guard their tongues a bit more

carefully. To pronounce that the horror of 9/11 was God's punishment on a sinful America was terribly hurtful and based on a misreading of the Old Testament. Pat Robertson once went on about some Haitian deal with the devil a couple of centuries ago that resulted in all the suffering there over the past couple of centuries, including the earthquake. Even if he believes such a thing, doesn't he understand how that falls on the ears and hearts of nonbelievers?

All of the apostle Paul's teachings about how Christians ought to behave boil down to this: (1) do what is a good witness to Christ and (2) do what builds up the body of Christ; (3) avoid what is a bad witness and (4) avoid what tears down the body of Christ.[85] That's it. If only all of us would heed Paul's teachings, there would be many fewer obstacles thrown up in the paths of nonbelievers.

Gandhi was quoted as saying, "I like your Christ, I do not like your Christians. Your Christians are so unlike your Christ." That sums up the attitude of a lot nonbelievers. If only we Christians were just more, well, Christian. What gives?

Who is in the pews?

With all that said, let's step back for bit of perspective on just who is in the pews.

---

[85] Years ago, I picked up this four-fold understanding of Paul's imperatives, but I can no longer remember from whom; my apologies to the creator of this interpretation. I've always found it to be very helpful and very much on the mark.

Approximately 75 percent of adult Americans self-identify as Christian. So the question is, are they all actually Christian in something other than name? To put it another way, are some of them "cultural Christians," who have a Christian heritage but have embraced only the label? That question begs another, "What's a Christian?"

The apostle Paul would say that a Christian is someone who has placed their faith, their trust, in Jesus Christ. Their badge of membership would read simply, "Faith in Christ."

Can we know who has faith in Christ? The answer is a straightforward "no, we can't." Goodness, we have trouble enough knowing the state of our own heart, much less someone else's.

So that's it? End of conversation? In a way, yes. The truth is that we can never make pronouncements on who is a Christian and who is not, for we can never know the nature of someone else's relationship with God.

C. S. Lewis wrote that he would sometimes meet a quite awful person who claimed to be a Christian and think to himself that the person couldn't possibly be a Christian. But then he came to realize that he didn't know just how awful the person would be without Jesus. He also realized that some people are nice by nature or upbringing, including many nonbelievers. How much more wonderful a person could they be, he thought to himself, if they came to know Christ.

But mustn't there be more to this? Doesn't how we live mean anything? Doesn't it say something about who we are and who we claim to be? To get at that, we need to first remind ourselves how one becomes a Christian.

Born from above

All Christians are new creations; "the old has gone and the new has come" (2 Cor. 5:17). Put another way, all those who have placed their faith in Christ have been born anew. And who creates? God, of course. This is God's work, not our own. Nobody helps along their own birth. That is Jesus' point to a Pharisee named Nicodemus in the first of this chapter's Scripture passages (John 3:1-10,16).

Jesus wants Nicodemus to grasp that being part of God's people and their entry into God's kingdom had never been about what Nicodemus had most valued: the Law, circumcision, the temple, the land. Instead, it had always been and still was about faith— faith that was possible only after the radical transformation, the rebirth, brought by the Spirit of God.

When we are "born of water and the Spirit," when we are cleansed and given new life, the transformation is total, reaching into every part of our being. This is not about adding something to us that was lacking. It is not about fixing something that was broken. It is not about any incremental approach. Rather, it is about our complete and utter rebirth, regeneration, re-creation.

Granted, we often don't act like the born-from-above people of God, much like a child who isn't acting his age. But the Spirit works with each of us so that as we mature in Christ, our thoughts, words, and actions increasingly conform to the new person God has created. All this, because God loves us so much that he gave his only Son on that cross, so we might be offered the new birth of water and the Spirit.

This rebirth of water and the Spirit is for each person. It can't be inherited from parents nor passed on from one generation to the next. The content of our faith can be taught and we can be good examples for our children, but being born from above must come to each person and, for some, it can come very late in life.

From birth to maturity

As a Christian, do we have any part to play in this? Not in the rebirth, but certainly in what comes after. You can think of our growth toward Christlikeness as a cooperative project, one needing both God and ourselves to work toward that goal. It is a process.

That is the point Paul makes in his letter to the Colossians, the second of this chapter's Scripture passages. He gives us a list of vices and a list of virtues. We are to set aside the one and embrace the other. We are to "put to death" the vices, the habitual sins, that separate us from God and "set our minds on things above." We are to shed our old lives and embrace our new lives. We are to strip off our old selves and put on our new selves.

Off with the old clothes, on with the new. Paul works this metaphor really hard. Why? Perhaps, Paul has in mind the baptism practices of the early church. Many of the Christians in the first century were converts from paganism and came into the Christian community as adults. Frequently, they would wear old clothes to the baptism and emerge from their immersion to put on a new set of white clothes, signifying the purity of the new life they were entering.[86]

When we put on this new life, this "new self, which is being renewed in knowledge according to the image of its creator" (v. 10), the transformation encompasses our whole being. Intellectually, we believe things that we didn't before, about ourselves, this world, about our purpose in life, and so on. Morally, we gain a different sense of right and wrong, of good and evil. Behaviors, thoughts, even TV shows and movies which once seemed harmless, no longer do. Emotionally, we love differently. We lavish less love upon ourselves and pour out our love upon God and one another. We become spiritually open to God, but also to the spiritual needs of others. We see the image of God in those whom we once ignored, or worse, oppressed.[87] The old has gone, the new has come (2 Corinthians 5:17). It is the complete reshaping of our core convictions and, hence, of how we think and live.

---

[86] From Tom Wright's, *Paul for Everyone: The Prison Letters* (Louisville, Ky.: Westminster John Knox Press, 2003).

[87] I've paraphrased some of this from John Stackhouse's book, *Humble Apologetics* (New York: Oxford University Press USA, 2002).

Though our rebirth is a gift from God, we still must learn to walk in the Spirit of Christ, to walk in God's way, to walk in a manner befitting the new clothes that we wear. Paul knows that we are talking about a process, not a moment. It is why he speaks of the new self as *being* renewed, in the same sense as our proclamation that God's kingdom has come *already*, but *not yet* in all its fullness. We have been renewed *and* we are being renewed. We have been saved *and* we are being saved.

Paul wrote to the Galatians in a similar vein, "If [since!] we live by the Spirit, let us also be guided by the Spirit" (Galatians 5:25). Even for those who have been "raised with Christ," getting rid of the old and putting on the new does not come naturally and left alone, we would fail. But we are not alone. Rather, God has provided a helper and comforter, the Holy Spirit, who guides us, guards us, and strengthens us so that we may truly become whole, complete, and mature disciples of Christ (Matthew 5:48).

Being a good witness to the love of God

Are 75 percent of adult Americans really Christian? I doubt it, but that is really about as far as I can go. I can't ever know where any person is in their relationship with the God revealed in Jesus Christ. How could I know who has been "born from above?" How could I gauge where anyone is in their project of conforming to the character of Christ? I have enough trouble understanding where I am.

Still, does the behavior of those who profess Christ often pose obstacles to those are looking in the window? Yes. And it is not a new problem. Paul himself told the Corinthian Christians to restrain their over-the-top enthusiastic tongues-speaking in worship because nonbelievers looking in would think they were crazy (1 Corinthians 14:23). It is still good advice that applies to much of what we do.

I can't know who is a "real Christian," but I do know this. We can help one another to understand what is a good witness to Jesus and what is not, what builds up the community of believers and what tears it down. And we can urge one another to live ever more holy lives.

Senate Chaplain Barry C. Black feels that the biggest challenge in his job is to be ethically congruent, i.e., to walk the talk—not only to profess and proclaim his faith in Christ, but to live it. "I have to make sure my actions match my rhetoric. I call it 'pass the private eye test' and 'being who you say you are.' Capitol Hill is a very seductive environment with money, power, and beautiful people. There are those who want to get to you because they feel you can help them get to others, so being the 'real deal' is critical."[88]

Perhaps the question we need to answer isn't "Who is a real Christian?" but "Am I the real deal?"

---

[88] From an interview in *Bible Study* magazine (January/February 2010), p. 13.

Is God a Bully?

Joshua 8:1-2, 18, 8:21-26 (NIV)

Then the LORD said to Joshua, "Do not be afraid; do not be discouraged. Take the whole army with you, and go up and attack Ai. For I have delivered into your hands the king of Ai, his people, his city and his land. ² You shall do to Ai and its king as you did to Jericho and its king, except that you may carry off their plunder and livestock for yourselves. Set an ambush behind the city."

¹⁸ Then the LORD said to Joshua, "Hold out toward Ai the javelin that is in your hand, for into your hand I will deliver the city." So Joshua held out toward the city the javelin that was in his hand.

²¹ For when Joshua and all Israel saw that the ambush had taken the city and that smoke was going up from it, they turned around and attacked the men of Ai. ²² Those in the ambush also came out of the city against them, so that they were caught in the middle, with Israelites on both sides. Israel cut them down, leaving them neither survivors nor fugitives. ²³ But they took the king of Ai alive and brought him to Joshua.

²⁴ When Israel had finished killing all the men of Ai in the fields and in the wilderness where they had chased them, and when every one of them had been put to the sword, all the Israelites returned to Ai and killed those who were in it. ²⁵ Twelve thousand men and women fell that day—all the

people of Ai. ²⁶ For Joshua did not draw back the hand that held out his javelin until he had destroyed all who lived in Ai.

Matthew 5:38-45 (NIV)

³⁸ "You have heard that it was said, 'Eye for eye, and tooth for tooth.' ³⁹ But I tell you, do not resist an evil person. If anyone slaps you on the right cheek, turn to them the other cheek also. ⁴⁰ And if anyone wants to sue you and take your shirt, hand over your coat as well. ⁴¹ If anyone forces you to go one mile, go with them two miles. ⁴² Give to the one who asks you, and do not turn away from the one who wants to borrow from you.

⁴³ "You have heard that it was said, 'Love your neighbor and hate your enemy.' ⁴⁴ But I tell you, love your enemies and pray for those who persecute you, ⁴⁵ that you may be children of your Father in heaven. He causes his sun to rise on the evil and the good, and sends rain on the righteous and the unrighteous.

John 1:29 (NIV)

²⁹ The next day John saw Jesus coming toward him and said, "Look, the Lamb of God, who takes away the sin of the world!"

1 John 4:9 (NIV)

⁹ This is how God showed his love among us: He sent his one and only Son into the world that we might live through him.

*The Old Testament seems to reveal a violent,
wrathful God who decrees even genocide. How could this possibly be
the same God revealed in Jesus? What is the Bible really saying
to us about who God is? Could God really be a bully?*

Given this topic, I wanted to find one over-the-top bloodthirsty
passage from the Old Testament. It was too easy an assignment.
I chose the massacre of Ai—all 12,000 men, women, and,
presumably children. Granted, Ai was a mortal enemy and
Canaan was to be the land for the Israelites, but this story
follows fast on the heels of the story of Jericho. There, not
only did the walls come a' tumblin' down, but every man,
woman, and child was put to death but Joshua and the Israelite
army (Joshua 6:21). All of it seemingly sanctioned by God.
As Robert Coote writes in his commentary on the book of
Joshua, "There is probably nothing in the Bible more offensive
to modern sensibilities than God's sanction of genocide against
the Canaanites."[89]

We shouldn't kid ourselves about how big a hurdle such Bible
stories pose to believers and nonbelievers alike. The prominent
neo-atheist, Richard Dawkins, recently wrote, "The God of
the Old Testament is arguably the most unpleasant character in
all fiction: jealous and proud of it; a petty, unjust, unforgiving
control-freak; a vindictive, bloodthirsty ethnic cleanser; a
misogynistic, homophobic, racist, infanticidal, genocidal,

---

[89] From Coote's commentary in Volume 2 of *The New Interpreters Bible*
published by Abingdon Press, 1998.

filicidal, pestilential, megalomaniacal, sadomasochistic, capriciously malevolent bully."[90]

Granted, it's the usual Dawkins stick-in-the-eye grotesque and offensive overstatement, but there is a small element of truth to it.

We can be forgiven for asking, "Who is this God we meet in the Old Testament? Where is the love? Where is the God who is revealed in Jesus?" I get asked that question a lot.

Marcion

In the middle of the second century, little more than a century after Jesus' death and resurrection, Marcion, a ship owner from Asia Minor, came to Rome and asked those very questions. His answer was to begin teaching a surprising brand of the Christian message. He believed that there was a total discontinuity between the Old Testament and the New, between the God of the Old Testament and Jesus, the God of the New Testament. Marcion wanted to get rid of the Old Testament entirely, believing that the god depicted in it was a lesser god and unworthy of Christian worship. Obviously, since the Hebrew Scriptures are part of every Bible, Marcion's ideas were rejected. He was even excommunicated. But the problem lingers. How could God sanction, even order, such genocidal warfare? Must Sodom and Gomorrah really have been completely and utterly

---

[90] From Dawkins's recent book, *The God Delusion* (New York: Mariner Books, 2008).

destroyed? Who is this God whose law seems to be an eye for an eye, at best, rather than turn the other cheek?

There are many facets to these questions; here's a few.

We need to remember that the ancient world was a harsh and violent place. Life was cheap. Slavery was common. I only half-jokingly ask my students to imagine living in the world of Conan the Barbarian. Then and now, God has to deal with us as we are, not as we wish we were.

In the ancient world, the kings were also the supreme warriors and commanders. Thus, we should expect that because the God of Israel was also to be their king, it is God who fills the role of warrior and commander. YHWH commands the armies that conquer Canaan; so long as the people follow YHWH's battle plans, they succeed. This imagery carries over to the New Testament as well. In Revelation, for example, Jesus is the divine warrior on the white horse, commanding the angel armies. It surprises people to learn that the "Lord of Hosts" is a military title; "hosts" is a term for armies.

Yet, there are countless examples in the Old Testament of God's love and mercy. Two of my favorites are Hosea 2:13-15 and Micah 6:6-8, both written hundreds of years before Jesus. Both prophets are from a time centuries before Jesus. How do we reconcile the warrior God depicted in Joshua and the forgiving, loving God depicted in Hosea?

Perhaps, the key that will open this up for us is to learn a bit about Scripture's developing revelation of the nature of God.

Progressive Revelation

When you first meet someone, do you know all there is to know about them? Of course not. You will come to know them over time, often a long time, and only to the extent that they open up and reveal themselves. We should count ourselves blessed if there is one person to whom we can reveal ourselves completely.

So it is with God. When Abraham first meets God, he learns something of who God is. But he doesn't seem to know God's name. God makes promises to Abraham, but he doesn't live to see those promises kept. Did he ever wonder whether God is as good at keeping promises as he is at making them?

Looking two millennia past Abraham, God isn't fully revealed until the coming of Jesus. The incarnation and Jesus' subsequent faithfulness to God and the covenant reveals to us that God is truly the great promise-keeper.[91] Likewise, before Jesus, none of God's people knew that God was inherently relational, the unity of one God made up of three persons: Father, Son, and Holy Spirit. Abraham and Moses and Elijah would never have imagined such a thing. Neither would we without Jesus. It is

---

[91] Katherine Grieb's excellent study of Romans, *The Story of Romans: A Narrative Defense of God's Righteousness* (Louisville, Ky., 2002), makes this point well. We don't normally think of God needing a defense, but in Jesus' day, many Jews wondered if God's promises would ever be fully kept. In his letter to the Romans, Paul makes the case that the very coming of Jesus and his faithfulness all the way to the cross demonstrates that God keeps the promises God makes.

Jesus who reveals to us that God not only loves but *is* love in God's very being.

Thus, we shouldn't be surprised that some aspects of God are revealed slowly in Scripture over time. It isn't that God is growing or changing; it is just that he is letting his people know more and more about him as they live with God over the centuries.

You might ask why God waits to reveal himself fully. Well, I think it is because God has to deal with us as we are. Here's an example of what I mean. In the Bible there is a developing revelation of forgiveness. I think you'll see the progression.

In Genesis 4:23-24, Lamech tells his wives that he will kill a young man for striking him. Lamech says he will be avenged seventy-seven times! Talk about unlimited vengeance. It is the world of Conan: You've killed my child, and now we are going to kill every man, woman, and child in your village.

In such a world, the "eye for an eye" of Exodus 21:23-25 is at least proportional vengeance. It sounds so harsh to our ears, but it is real moral progress over the seventy-seven-fold vengeance of Lamech.

Indeed, Leviticus 19:18 (still in the Law of Moses) says "you shall not take vengeance or bear a grudge against any of your people." And in Deuteronomy, 32:35, God says "Vengeance is mine." Much the same is repeated in Proverbs 20:22. Vengeance is still in the picture, but now it is to be handed over to God.

And, finally, God's desires for us are fully revealed by Jesus. In Matthew 5:38, Jesus takes the law from "an eye for an eye" to turning the other cheek and going the second mile. And when Peter asks Jesus how many times he should forgive, Jesus tells him seventy-seven times,[92] the perfect reversal of Lamech's desire for vengeance (Matthew 18:21-22).

It comes down to this, as it does in all things theological: Jesus is the full and complete revelation of God. When we see Jesus, we see God. When Jesus teaches, it is God teaching.

There are different ways of coming at the questions of God's depiction in the Old Testament. Perhaps, in the light of Christ, we are supposed to understand that the Hebrew writers ascribe actions to God that aren't really God's. Perhaps when Moses announces that God has instructed him to roar through the Israelite camp slaughtering thousands, it is Moses's anger on display, not God's.

But perhaps not. Perhaps we are supposed to understand that in that time and in that place God merely did what had to be done to preserve and protect a people, so that all the families of the earth could be blessed through them.

Perhaps ... perhaps ... there is no end to the perhaps. The Bible always has and always will pose enormous interpretive challenges. The bumper sticker "The Bible says it; I believe it"

---

[92] In the Greek this can also be translated "seventy times seven," trumping Lamech's vengeance tenfold.

just isn't helpful. What does the Bible really say? What does God intend for us to hear?

Through it all, we know this: God is no bully. God is not vindictive. God is not unjust or unforgiving. God is neither capricious nor megalomaniacal. How do we know this? Because we know Jesus. The one in the "form of God" who "emptied himself, taking the form of a slave." The one who "humbled himself and became obedient to the point of death—even death on a cross" (Philippians 2:7-8).

Hell?

Psalm 49:13-15 (NIV)

¹³ This is the fate of those who trust in themselves,
    and of their followers, who approve their sayings.
  ¹⁴ They are like sheep and are destined to die;
    death will be their shepherd
    (but the upright will prevail over them in the
      morning).
  Their forms will decay in the grave,
    far from their princely mansions.
  ¹⁵ But God will redeem me from the realm of the dead;
    he will surely take me to himself.

Matthew 8:10-12 (NIV)

¹⁰ When Jesus heard this, he was amazed and said to those following him, "Truly I tell you, I have not found anyone in Israel with such great faith. ¹¹ I say to you that many will come from the east and the west, and will take their places at the feast with Abraham, Isaac and Jacob in the kingdom of heaven. ¹² But the subjects of the kingdom will be thrown outside, into the darkness, where there will be weeping and gnashing of teeth."

1 Peter 3:18-20 (NIV)

¹⁸ For Christ also suffered once for sins, the righteous for the unrighteous, to bring you to God. He was put to death in

the body but made alive in the Spirit. [19] After being made alive, he went and made proclamation to the imprisoned spirits—[20] to those who were disobedient long ago when God waited patiently in the days of Noah while the ark was being built. In it only a few people, eight in all, were saved through water....

Revelation 20:11-15 (NIV)

[11] Then I saw a great white throne and him who was seated on it. The earth and the heavens fled from his presence, and there was no place for them. [12] And I saw the dead, great and small, standing before the throne, and books were opened. Another book was opened, which is the book of life. The dead were judged according to what they had done as recorded in the books. [13] The sea gave up the dead that were in it, and death and Hades gave up the dead that were in them, and each person was judged according to what they had done. [14] Then death and Hades were thrown into the lake of fire. The lake of fire is the second death. [15] Anyone whose name was not found written in the book of life was thrown into the lake of fire.

For a topic that gets as much attention in our world as hell, Christians seem to either talk about it too much or not at all. What is the biblical understanding of hell? What are some of our misconceptions? And, most importantly, what if anything does it have to do with the Good News?

And so we come to the last topic that often is thrown up to Christians. Certainly, many nonbelievers object to the notion of hell. And even among Christians, this topic gets widely varied reactions. Over the last 2,000 years, more than a few Christians almost seemed to revel in their belief that everlasting fires would forever torment those who reject Jesus. Other Christians are simply repelled by the whole notion and can't find much of Jesus in it. So, there are a few things that we need to keep in mind as we come to this difficult and contentious topic.

First, this is an intramural argument, i.e., one amongst believers. On my shelves is a book entitled, *Four Views of Hell: Literal, Metaphorical, Purgatorial, Conditional* (Zondervan, 1996), containing four quite different views of hell from four well-respected biblical scholars. They very much disagree with one another, but they would acknowledge that all are Christian and that none are heretics.[93] Tough topics, like the ones that we've been tackling in this section call for us to pour a lot of grace out upon one another, recognizing that we won't all agree. We'll still be debating this and many topics up till the day Jesus returns.

Second, there is some important background we need to bring to the topic and even some "unlearning" we need to do.

---

[93] Heresy refers to destructive and destabilizing distortions of the faith. Disputes about the nature of hell haven't typically been labeled as heresies in the Christian community. The heresies that gave rise to the writing of the great Christian creeds revolved around the nature and person of Jesus.

Much of what we think we know about hell comes from Dante's *Inferno* and Milton's *Paradise Lost*. These are enormously imaginative and powerful works that have laid claim to the cultural psyche. It takes some effort to come to a topic like hell with a blank slate, but if we are going to read Scripture well, we must try.

In the cosmology of the ancient world, the gods are "up there," the living are here on the ground, and the dead are down below, under the ground. This was true for the Greeks and the Jews alike. The above passage from Psalm 49 refers to Sheol which, you'll recall, was the name given by the Jews to the place of the dead: "down there," the "underworld" some might call it. There was little sense of it being a place of punishment. Rather, it was the place where the dead are. The Greek name for this place was "Hades." There are sixty-five references in the Old Testament to Sheol and ten references in the New Testament to Hades. Again, it is crucial to grasp that these were not generally understood to be places of punishment. Shadowy and creepy, yes, but not punishment.[94]

In the above passage from 1 Peter, the "spirits in prison" simply refers to the dead. It is a prison because one can't come back from there, but there is no connotation of burning fires or other forms of punishment. And notice in the passage exactly who it is that Jesus is going to visit—the folks who were so wicked that

---

[94] In Jewish writings from around the time of Jesus (e.g., *Wisdom of Solomon* and *1 Enoch*), we can see the development of the idea of eternal torment for the wicked. It is important to understand that these writings are not part of the Old Testament canon.

God wiped out the planet with a flood and started over. These are certainly not the faithful departed, such as Abraham.

There are thirteen references in the New Testament to hell, which is different than Hades. Of these, eleven come from the mouth of Jesus.[95] Hell translates the Greek word *gehenna* and refers to an actual place.

The best known biblical image for hell derives from a deep, narrow gorge southeast of Jerusalem called *gê ben hinnōm*, "the Valley of Ben Hinnom," in which idolatrous Israelites offered up child sacrifices to the gods Molech and Baal (2 Chronicles 28:3; 33:6; Jeremiah 7:31-32; 19:2-6). Josiah defiled the valley to make it unacceptable as a holy site (2 Kings 23:10), after which it was used as a garbage dump by the inhabitants of Jerusalem. As a result, the Valley of Ben Hinnom became known as the dump heap, the place of destruction by fire in Jewish tradition. The Greek word *gehenna*, 'hell,' commonly used in the New Testament for the place of final punishment, is derived from the Hebrew name for this valley."[96]

Because Jesus is referring to the ever-burning garbage dump of Jerusalem, we have to keep in mind that Jesus' warnings are centered on what will happen to his fellow Jews if they do not abandon the course they are on and embrace Jesus' way and the

---

[95] The count is only seven if we eliminate duplicates from parallels in the synoptic gospels.

[96] Ryken, L., Wilhoit, J., Longman, T., Duriez, C., Penney, D., & Reid, D. G., *Dictionary of Biblical Imagery* (electronic ed.) (Downers Grove, Ill.: InterVarsity Press, 2000), 376.

coming of God's kingdom. They did not, and forty years later the Romans burned Jerusalem, piling countless Jewish bodies into the fiery horrors of Gehanna.

So, is there a hell?

Because the word "hell" is so loaded with emotion and misconceptions, let's begin with this question: *Will there be those who do not enjoy eternal life with Christ?*

The vast majority of Christians over the last 2,000 years would answer "yes." There are some universalists who believe that all those who have ever lived will in the end be saved and reconciled with God. And this group has probably been growing in recent decades. But, historically, this belief has often been seen as outright heresy. Two early church fathers, Origen and Gregory of Nyssa, apparently affirmed their belief in universalism. But it was condemned as heresy by the Second Council of Constantinople in AD 553. The great theologian, Karl Barth, seemed to embrace this belief, at least at times. And the influential theologian, Jurgen Moltmann, certainly does.[97] I even have on my shelves a book titled *The Evangelical Universalist*, which seems like an oxymoron and explains why it was published anonymously, even though written by an obviously knowledgeable New Testament scholar.

In my view, the belief that all will be saved, regardless of their free desires, is heretical, in that it significantly distorts

---

[97] From Roger Olson's, *The Mosaic of Christian Belief: Twenty Centuries of Unity and Diversity* (Downers Grove, Ill.: InterVarsity Press, 2004).

the gospel by eliminating the need for our love of God, our faith and trust in God, to be freely given. And love isn't really love if it is not freely given. At the great judgment depicted in Revelation 20, there are those whose names are found the book of life and those whose names are not. The latter are "thrown into the lake of fire." The question of "hell" revolves around what happens to them, to those not in the book of life.

Okay, what happens to those who will not enjoy eternal life with Christ?

One answer might be that they are tossed into that lake of fire in Rev. 20:15, where one might presume they would be burned up, annihilated, for that is what fire does. Or perhaps they head for the "outer darkness" of Matthew 8:12. That certainly evokes the chaos and desolation of an existence without God, which I hesitate to even call "life." Something like the eternal grayness imagined by C.S. Lewis.

Or perhaps, it is a place where those who deny God spend eternity suffering in a fire that burns but doesn't consume so that "the smoke of their torment goes up forever and ever" and their torment is "in the presence of the holy angels and of the Lamb [Jesus]" (see Rev. 14:9-11).[98] In the fourth century, Augustine went so far as to speculate that God uses his creative power to ensure that there is always fresh flesh for burning.[99] As you might guess, many find it hard to picture Jesus condoning such torment even of the very worst among those who deny him.

You can see the problem. It really isn't surprising that there is a book outlining four quite different views of hell by knowledgeable and well-meaning Christians. I'm guessing there are quite a few such books. The Bible just doesn't give us all the answers we seek.

Over the years, there have been two thoughts around this topic that have not let go of me. The first is from Clark Pinnock, an evangelical biblical scholar who has gotten into some hot water with his more conservative colleagues on this topic. Pinnock simply pointed out that (1) the phrase in Scripture is "eternal punishment," not "eternal punishing," and (2) fire would consume and destroy even resurrected bodies, which are still flesh and bone.

---

[98] I'll simply note here that you don't have to spend much time in Revelation to realize it would be absurd to hold that all the images in this apocalyptic writing are "photographic" depictions of actual events in the past, present, or future. Will we one day live in a city made of pure gold? And, if so, how could it be clear as glass? (Rev. 21:18). To treat the glories of Revelation in that way is to abuse this God-breathed writing and to miss the point entirely.

[99] Book 21 of Augustine's *City of God*.

Pinnock found himself led by Scripture to the belief that those who, in the end, choose against God will simply cease to exist, i.e., they will be annihilated. But, you might say, aren't our souls immortal? Although this tends to be how Christians understand things, it really isn't necessarily a biblical concept. At least, I've never been able to find it in Scripture.[100] We are not promised eternal life outside our life with God.

N. T. Wright asks us to consider this. We are made in the image of God. Sadly, too many peoples' lives are devoted to pursuits and purposes that chip away at it, much like a statue that is allowed to accumulate rust and slowly decay. Until we are reconciled to God, this image of God continues to deteriorate. Indeed some people commit such horrors that we wonder if there is anything of God left in them.

What happens if a person never comes to faith in Christ in this life or, possibly, even the next? Would not the image of God in them finally be extinguished? And, if so, what remains of their humanity? Of all God's creatures, only we humans are made in his image. What if that image were gone? Could we even be considered human? Would we not be just another beast? Immortal perhaps, but no longer "Scott," no longer a person, no longer human.

---

[100] It is fascinating how many such beliefs there are. We assume that they are in the Bible, but they have actually come from elsewhere and we've then simply strived to make them fit. Many such imported ideas come from Plato.

In the end, we affirm that we have been created to live in loving fellowship with God and one another. The life for which we have been made is a life with God. And it is in God alone that we find true life. As in almost all topics around the "Last Things" we have many more questions than we do answers. Perhaps it is this way so that we will focus on our relationship with God and hear well his charge to proclaim, by word and deed, God's good news to all who will listen. All the rest of it … well, we get to leave that in God's hands, for which we should be eternally thankful!

Getting Past Christian-ish

Is hitting that Restart button enough? The truth is that this book is only a beginning. You've gotten this far, and the question on your mind might be "So what?" Getting past Christian-ish is not just about learning, it is as much about doing.

First, if you are not part of a church, then find one and start going ... and then keep going. Getting past Christian-ish isn't something you could ever really do on your own. You might make a wholehearted start, but you'll find that lasting transformation takes friends and fellow travelers.

If you are part of a church and you go regularly, your church may not be as much help as you'd like or expect. It is a "flux capacitor" problem.

In her book, *Almost Christian*, Kenda Creasy Dean[101] likens much church ministry to the famous flux capacitor in the movie *Back to the Future*. Marty McFly has found himself in 1955, and he will stay there unless 1955-Doc figures out how to use 1985-Doc's much-modified DeLorean to get Marty back where he belongs. The problem is that it takes 1.21 "jigowatts" of power flowing into the DeLorean's flux capacitor to make the jump back. Where are they ever going to get that much energy? And harness it in a single moment? The brilliant idea

---

[101] Dean's book is a preacher's treasure trove, chock full of great illustrations, metaphors, and phrases.

is to harness a lightning bolt. The problem is that they have to get the car to precisely the right place at precisely the right time to make it work.

And that, Dean suggests, is how we too often see our various church ministries—as flux capacitors. If we can get just the right programs to go along with powerful sermons and vibrant small groups we'll create some "holy fire." But, as Dean succinctly puts it:

> The delusion that human effort can generate mature faith—in young people or in anybody else—is old as fiction itself. Trying to channel God, like trying to channel lightning, kept countless false prophets in business throughout the Hebrew scriptures. Today, we are more likely to view God as a source of fuel than a source of awe as we try to harness divine power for our own use. But ancient people had it right: they hid their faces at the Lord's approach, and prayed for mercy.

The apostle Paul agrees with Dean. In his letter to the believers in Ephesus, Paul proclaims that we have been put right with God (saved) by his grace, not by anything we have done. God's grace and grace alone. *Sola gratia!* as the Protestant reformers had printed on their bumper stickers.

The hard-to-face truth is that we don't create faith in ourselves or in anyone else. When John Wesley's heart was strangely warmed, it was God doing the warming, not the preacher. Despite many extravagant claims, no preacher has ever saved a single soul. It is God who saves, not we. We may like to be in charge and in control, but we aren't.

So ... what do we actually do then? Just wait for God to do God's thing? Find a comfortable easy chair and pass the time? Just hang out until God hits the switch? Or to put it in more Bible-sounding terms, do we pray and then wait patiently on the Lord?

Dry kindling

We can't set our own hearts afire, but we are real good at dousing them with cold water. Ever been "tuned out" by your own kids? Ever felt drowned out by the noise of your teenager's life? I imagine God feels much the same way at times.

Thus, Dean hits on a very apt metaphor when she suggests that, although we can't set our own hearts on fire, we can make ourselves *highly combustible*. We can shape ourselves into dry kindling, which even a tenderfoot knows catches fire much more easily than a pile of wet, green wood.

How do we make ourselves highly combustible? Here too, the apostle Paul is helpful. Using an ever-popular sports metaphor (after all, guys are guys), Paul tells the Christians in Corinth that they have chosen a life that takes training, not merely trying. And certainly not waiting around in an easy chair for God to light a match.

When trying is not enough

In his book, *The Life You've Always Wanted* (Zondervan, 2002), John Ortberg, too, uses a sports metaphor. Suppose you woke up tomorrow morning and decided to run a marathon. You put on some running shoes, don the right apparel, and head out the door to begin your 26.2 mile run. Could you do it? What if you tried hard? Really, really hard? If you gave it the ole' 110 percent? The obvious answer is no, of course not. No matter how hard I tried, I couldn't simply head out the door and run 26 miles. If I want to run a marathon, I'm going to have to train for it. Effort alone won't cut it. I once taught people to fly jet airplanes. There again, effort was essential, but it took a year of hard training to create an Air Force pilot. Nobody flies a jet by effort alone the first time they try, or the second, or the tenth. They train for it.

So it is with all the great endeavors of our lives. It takes learning and training and practice. And what could be a greater endeavor than becoming the person God has created each of us to be, a passionate servant of our Lord Jesus Christ, with the power "to work the works of the kingdom," as Dallas Willard put it.

When Paul wrote to the Christians in Corinth, he was training hard in the things of God. He knew that without training, we would never become highly combustible dry kindling.

Too often, Christians make the mistake of thinking that this is a one-and-done game: "I believe in Jesus; now it is time to get back to real life." But nothing could be further from the truth.

Embracing Jesus with our heart, mind, soul, and strength could never be about "getting our ticket punched." The Jesus Way is a lifelong pursuit.

Training for the fruit

Of course, it is one thing to say we are going to train ourselves to be more highly combustible, but it's another to know how. In his letter to the Galatians, Paul tells the Christians that those who are led by the Spirit will bear the fruit of the Spirit: "love, joy, peace, patience, kindness, generosity, faithfulness, gentleness, and self-control." But how do you train yourself to be gentle or to be joyful? I can *try* to be patient (boy, have I tried … and failed), but how do I *train* myself to be patient?

Ortberg knows that he needs to slow down if he is going to embrace the life God offers him. But he also acknowledges that he suffers from "hurry-up sickness." I know just what he means. I make a careful and complex calculation as I arrive with my basket at the grocery store checkout. I scan the lines, estimate the speed of the checkers, note which lines have a dedicated bagger, and, after factoring in estimated tender times (carefully judging the number of check writers), I select my line and then, too often, end up enormously frustrated because my "competition" (the person standing in my place in the line I didn't choose) gets out faster than I do. My wife, Patti, and I have been known to stand in two ticket lines at the movies. Whoever gets to the window first buys the tickets! Yes, it is a sickness. After all, what do I really do with those five minutes I might save? Surely less than I imagine.

How do I possibly learn patience? How do I learn to slow down and catch my breath? Ortberg has tried picking the longest line on purpose, hoping he'd learn to like it. I haven't yet worked up the strength of will to emulate his training method. But I do know that if I don't actually train myself to be more patient, I won't ever get there. Yes, God helps me in this, but I must still learn to be patient.

How about prayer? Christians with deep and meaningful prayer lives didn't arrive there by accident. They learned to pray. They trained to pray. They were disciplined, praying even when they didn't feel like it or thought they had nothing to say. The same with Bible reading and study. At St. Andrew, we read through the entire Bible a few years ago. Those who completed the *Thru the Bible* reading program did so because they were disciplined and determined, reading even if they didn't feel like it, learning a method that would get them to their goal. Have you ever taken a Bible study with other Christians, or are you still just trying on your own to discover the life-changing power of Scripture?

This is no time for resting comfortably in an easy chair. American Christianity has been too comfortable for too long. It is time to move, to get going.

Yes, it is God who sets our hearts on fire. Yes, our salvation is a gift. But there is also work for us in God's rescue. Making ourselves highly combustible, ready to ignite with God's spark, is our part in this.

The question is this: "Will we?" Will we just tiptoe into these waters or are we ready to go all-in?

Appendix

Practical Bible Study Tools

Study Bibles

At St. Andrew we generally use two translations: the New Revised Standard Version (NRSV)[102] and the new 2011 revision of the New International Version (NIV). Both are good, reliable translations and are available in a wide variety of study Bible editions.

In most of these study Bibles below, the study notes are principally oriented to explaining the historical and cultural context of biblical passages, rather than offering a theological interpretation of them. A caution: it is all too natural for us to begin to see the theology of the notes' authors as our own, giving it undue authority. The Scofield and Ryrie study Bibles are examples of study Bibles with a theological mission, and I don't recommend either.

NIV Study Bible (copyright 2011). This is the latest update of a longtime favorite and uses the new revision of the NIV. It is loaded with footnotes of all sorts. There are also many

---

[102] NRSV Bibles are often available with the books of the Apocrypha or without. The Apocrypha is a set of Jewish writings from the period between the Old and New Testaments. They can be very helpful in understanding Jesus' world.

maps and charts. The footnotes are written from a conservative viewpoint (in most places that doesn't really matter). This Bible is fully four-color, pointing the way ahead for other publishers. The iPad version is a well-done implementation with all the content of the print version.

The Access Bible: An Ecumenical Learning Resource for People of Faith, 1999, Oxford University Press (NRSV). The book introductions are not at all intimidating, and the study notes are largely embedded in the text. This study Bible also includes a simple glossary of key biblical terms, maps, tables of weights and measures (what is a cubit?!), and a concise concordance. (A concordance shows the various verse locations for key words in the Bible. For example, the concordance in this study Bible includes six verses where the word "help" can be found.)

The Renovare Spiritual Formation Bible, 2005, Harper San Francisco (NRSV). This is an excellent reading Bible, filled with comments and supplements aimed at helping the reader engage Scripture for spiritual development. It is not really a study Bible in that it has very limited study helps and cross-references. This one makes an excellent supplement to a study Bible.

The New Interpreter's Study Bible, 2003, Abingdon Press (NRSV). It is stuffed with study notes that are written with a pastoral orientation, rather than being strictly scholarly. It also has a number of brief essays that are part of the study notes. There are also six general articles on interpretation of the Bible. There is a glossary, chronology tables, and a full set of color maps. Although a paperback version was published at one time, it is currently available only in leather and hardcover bindings. This Bible is published only with the Apocrypha.

The New Oxford Annotated Bible, Fourth Edition, 2010, Oxford University Press (NRSV). The study notes are extensive and are embedded in book outlines at the bottom of each page. There is an index to the study materials (notes and essays), as well as a concise concordance and maps. This Bible also contains several essays on topics ranging from the history of the Bible's development to important cultural contexts of the Bible. There are also various timelines, tables of weights and measures, and more of the usual.

Basic tools

A good Bible dictionary is probably the single most helpful tool. I'd suggest the *Harper-Collins Bible Dictionary*, edited by Paul Achtemeier. This is a 1,250-page volume with more than 3,700 entries. It also provides a useful set of maps. This dictionary is probably the most used single volume in my library. The *New Bible Dictionary* is another excellent choice.

Your second purchase ought to be a good Bible atlas, as it helps to clear up a lot of confusion. *The IVP Atlas of Bible History* is excellent, as is the *Holman Bible Atlas*. I use both.

Another basic tool is a concordance. A Bible concordance lists all the words in the Bible in alphabetical order and provides the chapter-and-verse location of each occurrence of each word. As you can imagine, an unabridged concordance is a big book! Fortunately, an abridged version is suitable for nearly all purposes. If you purchase one, be sure to purchase one that is based on the translation you use most often for study, e.g., the NRSV or NIV. Bear in mind that a concordance has to be used thoughtfully, in that many English words are synonyms and they will all be listed under a single heading. If you use the NRSV, you can pick up John Kohlenberger's *The Concise Concordance to the NRSV*, 1993, Oxford Press. He has also prepared a concordance for the new NIV (copyright 2011).

Very helpful

Closing the cultural distance between biblical times and our own can be very difficult, but it is absolutely critical to useful Bible study. The entire Bible is culturally conditioned, and our understanding is much richer when we know more about the cultural, historical, geographical, and literary context of each book and passage. There is a commentary that goes through the Bible, passage by passage, giving the layperson important cultural background. For example, when Jesus told his disciples not to pray like the pagans (Matthew 6:7-8), it is very helpful to know how the pagans did pray. Or, why did Paul expect Corinthian women to cover their heads? This commentary is in two volumes: *The IVP Bible Background Commentary, Old Testament*, by Walton, Matthews, and Cavalas, 2000, InterVarsity Press. *The IVP Bible Background Commentary, New Testament*, by Craig Keener, 1993, InterVarsity Press.

The *NIV Archeological Study Bible* is also filled with lots of helpful and interesting information, photos, and maps. The publishers call it an illustrated walk through biblical history and culture, and it comes close to that.

Also helpful is a one-volume commentary on the Bible. A commentary will give you an overview of a chapter-by-chapter discussion of each book. I'd suggest the *HarperCollins Bible Commentary*, the companion volume to the *HarperCollins Bible Dictionary*. The *New Bible Commentary* is also helpful.

One of the difficulties in Bible study is figuring out how to pronounce all those strange names and words in the Bible. If you'd like some help with this, I suggest *The HarperCollins Bible Pronunciation Guide*, 1989, HarperCollins Publishers. This slim volume also contains nonbiblical terms that are important in the study of the Bible.

Helpful

Learning something about the Hebrew and Greek words that underlie our English translations can enrich your bible study. Though in-depth study can be difficult without knowledge of the original languages, various tools can help the layperson tackle fruitful word studies. The best starting point is *Mounce's Complete Expository Dictionary of Old and New Testament Words*, 2006, Zondervan. It is actually several dictionaries in a single volume. The Scripture index is very helpful, and there are many insights packed into the word discussions.

About the Author

Scott Engle is the Teaching Pastor at St. Andrew United Methodist Church, a vibrant and growing congregation of nearly 7,000 in Plano, Texas, just north of Dallas. Scott has been on staff at St. Andrew more than ten years, teaching numerous adult Bible studies during that time. Scott preaches most Sundays in one or more of St. Andrew's traditional services and serves on St. Andrew's executive team.

Scott began his professional career as a USAF pilot and then spent twenty-five years leading a variety of businesses, large and small. He has also taught at Texas Christian University and the University of North Texas. Scott holds a B.A. from Louisiana Tech University, an MBA from Harvard Business School, and a Ph.D. from the University of North Texas.

Scott and his wife, Patti, have been married fifteen years and make their home in Frisco, Texas. Between them, they have three grown sons and two grandsons.